FLIGHT

FLIGHT
100 GREATEST AIRCRAFT

MARK PHELPS

Edited by
ROBERT GOYER

weldon**owen**

CONTENTS

Introduction | 7

What's Your Favorite Airplane? | 8

Aircraft Basics | 10

Wright Flyer | 14

Douglas DC-3 | 17

Airbus A380 | 18

Piper J-3 Cub | 20

Beechcraft Starship | 22

Yakovlev Yak-9 | 24

Cessna 195 | 26

Ercoupe | 27

Boeing 314 Clipper | 29

Pitts Special | 30

Aerodynamic Advances | 32

Cessna Citation I | 34

Boeing B-17 Flying Fortress | 37

Bensen B-8 Gyrocopter | 38

Canadair CRJ | 40

Lockheed Martin F-22 Raptor | 43

Boeing-Stearman PT-17 Biplane | 44

Piper PA-46 Malibu | 46

Diamond DA40 | 47

Supermarine Spitfire | 48

AH-64 Apache | 50

TBM 700/800/850 | 53

North American F-86 Sabre | 54

Albatros D-Series | 56

Aviat Husky | 58

McDonnell Douglas F-15 Eagle | 61

Learjet 23 | 63

Engine Innovations | 64

Junkers Ju-52 | 67

North American AT-6 Texan | 69

Spirit of St. Louis | 70

Piper PA-32 Cherokee Six | 72

Quicksilver MX-2 | 73

Mitsubishi A6M Zero | 74

Aero Commander | 77

Kitfox | 78

Dassault Falcon 7X | 80

Vought F4U Corsair | 82

Northrop Grumman B-2 Stealth Bomber | 84

Gossamer Albatross | 86

Extra 300 | 88

Cessna CitationJet | 90

Mikoyan-Gurevich MiG-15 | 92

Cessna 210/P210 | 94

Gulfstream G650 | 96

Cessna 182 Skylane | 97

Antonov An-225 Mriya | 98

Granville Brothers Gee Bee R Series | 101

Piper PA-28 Cherokee | 103

Messerschmitt Bf 109 | 104

Sopwith Camel | 106

Beechcraft Staggerwing | 108

Lockheed SR-71 Blackbird | 110

Curtiss JN-4 Jenny | 112
Beechcraft Bonanza | 114
Boeing B-52 Stratofortress | 116
Cessna 208 Caravan | 119
Robinson R22 | 120
Boeing 737 | 122
Van's RVs | 124
Mooney M20 Series | 125
Lockheed P-38 Lightning | 126
Blériot XI | 129
Hindenburg | 131
BAe Harrier | 133
Heroes of Aviation | 134
Cessna Citation X | 136
Luscombe Model 8 Silvaire | 139
Piaggio Aero P.180 Avanti | 141
Ford Tri-Motor | 143
Cessna 172 Skyhawk | 145
North American P-51 Mustang | 146

Hawker Sea Fury | 149
Hawker Siddeley HS-125 | 150
Space Shuttle | 153
Cirrus SR22 | 154
Bede BD-5 | 155
Lockheed Constellation | 156
Lockheed C-130 Hercules | 158
de Havilland DHC-2 Beaver | 161
Wonders in Avionics | 162
Fokker Dr.1 Triplane | 164
Curtiss Model D | 167
Eclipse 500 | 168
Boeing B-29 Superfortress | 170
SPAD S.XIII | 173
Boeing 747 | 174
Lockheed 10/12 Electra | 177
Bell X-1 | 178
Aeronca Champ | 181
Bell-Boeing V-22 Osprey | 183

Bombardier Global Express | 185
Beechcraft King Air | 186
Pilatus PC-12 | 189
Consolidated B-24 Liberator | 190
General Atomics Predator Drone | 193
March of Aviation | 194
Embraer Phenom 100 | 196
Voyager | 198
McDonnell Douglas F-4 Phantom | 200
Cessna 150/152 | 202
Aérospatiale-BAC Concorde | 205
Messerschmitt Me 262 | 207
Beechcraft Baron | 208
Sukhoi SU-27 | 211

Specifications | 213
Acknowledgments | 239

INTRODUCTION

Only a handful of times since the dawn of the human race has a single technology changed the course of history as much as the aircraft. It has changed human mobility so profoundly that it's hard for those of us younger than a century old to envision a world without powered human flight. The global community, with all of its woes and wonders, was made possible and continues to be sustained by flight.

This book, simply entitled *Flight*, was inspired by a spectacularly popular selection of the top 100 aircraft of all time that the staff at *Flying* magazine created and unveiled online. In *Flight*, authored by Mark Phelps and shepherded expertly by Bethany Whitfield and Lucie Parker, we have taken the body and spirit of that original product and refined it, with stunning photography, expanded aircraft descriptions, and many additional features, including a look at many of the surrounding technologies that allowed humble airplanes, like the *Wright Flyer*—odd-shaped and barely capable of short, low flights—to evolve into supersonic marvels, like the Space Shuttle, capable of carrying people to space before gliding back home.

Creating *Flight* took a lot of work, but was ultimately a labor of love, since we are all pilots and simply love aircraft of all shapes and sizes. We do have our favorites, and the task of choosing among them inspired spirited discussion and sometimes equally spirited disagreement among us. Luckily, it was all part of the fun.

In selecting our list of the best flying machines in history, we realized almost immediately that it would be impossible not to leave out some fan favorites, so we focused on selecting aircraft that were somehow different from the pack, like the Piper Cub, which became an icon for personal flight, or the North American P-51, which played a big part in bringing a great war to an end. When you read *Flight*, you'll see that every airplane, helicopter, rocket plane, or dirigible we feature is indeed a special machine.

Ultimately, this is the story of those machines. There are models meek and mighty, from the cute little homemade Kitfox to the stately Douglas DC-3, and aircraft both fanciful and daring, from the human powered Gossamer Albatross to the roaring Gee Bee racer. All of them share the distinction of having contributed in their own way to the rich, dramatic, and endlessly intriguing story of flight.

Robert Goyer
Editor-in-Chief
of *Flying* Magazine

WHAT'S YOUR FAVORITE AIRPLANE?

It's a question all pilots have been asked. But "What are the top 100 airplanes in history?" doesn't usually come up in light conversation. However, if you were to pass out pencils and paper to a roomful of airplane geeks and ask them to draw up their lists, I'm confident that you'd end up with some pretty interesting reading.

There are plenty of stalwarts that will likely be on any aviation enthusiast's top 100 list—some because they achieved impressive technological feats, such as Charles Lindbergh's modified Ryan monoplane *The Spirit of St. Louis* or today's F-35 Joint Strike Fighter. Pioneering airliners that surely deserve a place on the roster include the Boeing 747, the Lockheed Constellation, and the Douglas DC-3. Collectively they transformed the first baby steps of global air travel into a safe, everyday routine. And personal aircraft—the best from Cessna, Piper, Beechcraft, Cirrus, and others—provide private individuals with their own magic carpets, whisking them above snarled surface traffic on business and pleasure flights.

So how did *we* choose which 100 airplanes are best? *Flying* Editor-in-Chief Robert Goyer said it was a challenging form of "aviation Sudoku." In my book, any machine that can take you up into the sky and safely back down again has got to be well above average when it comes to rating man-made contrivances. In fact, there are legions of amateur builders who rivet, weld, and glue their own airplanes together in garages, basements, and backyard workshops, and a few of those designs have certainly earned their place among the top 100. But some of history's more conventionally designed and manufactured airplanes also stand out, and you'll see them within these pages. In some cases, it's less about the machine and more about the people who gave it life. Sometimes, it's all about aesthetics. Maybe it's the airplane's extraordinary capability in a very specialized role, like bush flying or competition aerobatics. Or maybe an airplane represents a giant leap in technology when everyone else at the time was taking baby steps.

So everyone has their own criteria for picking the best. And any list like this one is guaranteed to start arguments. Everyone probably has a personal favorite that did not make this list. And I'm poised for the inevitable: "How on earth could you have left out the . . . ?" On the other hand, there are probably also a few aircraft that some might not agree belong in this distinguished company. I can hear it now: "The [fill in the blank] was a turkey and never should have made it off the drawing board!"

In the end, this book is meant as a celebration. To anyone who has known the joy of looking down on Earth from the domain of the birds, the wonder of *Flight* is what it's all about.

Mark Phelps

AIRCRAFT BASICS

The aircraft included in this book are all stellar examples of engineering innovation—from two-seater single-engine hobbyist fliers to brazen and bold military marvels, and from enormous corporate jets to some of the world's more modest yet no less cutting-edge small aircraft. Many of them share design elements, while some have unique features that help them do their specific jobs.

BASIC SINGLE-ENGINE AIRCRAFT

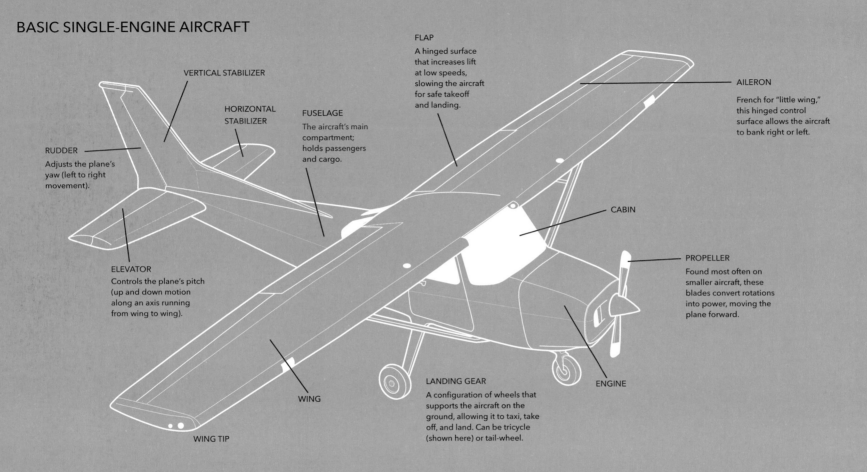

VERTICAL STABILIZER

HORIZONTAL STABILIZER

FUSELAGE
The aircraft's main compartment; holds passengers and cargo.

RUDDER
Adjusts the plane's yaw (left to right movement).

ELEVATOR
Controls the plane's pitch (up and down motion along an axis running from wing to wing).

WING

WING TIP

FLAP
A hinged surface that increases lift at low speeds, slowing the aircraft for safe takeoff and landing.

AILERON
French for "little wing," this hinged control surface allows the aircraft to bank right or left.

RADOME

CABIN

PROPELLER
Found most often on smaller aircraft, these blades convert rotations into power, moving the plane forward.

ENGINE

LANDING GEAR
A configuration of wheels that supports the aircraft on the ground, allowing it to taxi, take off, and land. Can be tricycle (shown here) or tail-wheel.

HELICOPTER

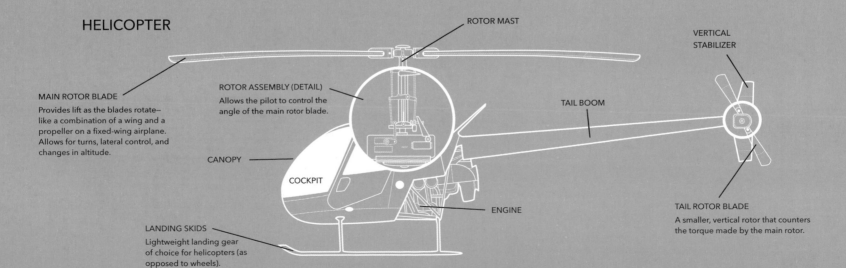

ROTOR MAST

MAIN ROTOR BLADE
Provides lift as the blades rotate—like a combination of a wing and a propeller on a fixed-wing airplane. Allows for turns, lateral control, and changes in altitude.

ROTOR ASSEMBLY (DETAIL)
Allows the pilot to control the angle of the main rotor blade.

CANOPY

COCKPIT

LANDING SKIDS
Lightweight landing gear of choice for helicopters (as opposed to wheels).

ENGINE

TAIL BOOM

VERTICAL STABILIZER

TAIL ROTOR BLADE
A smaller, vertical rotor that counters the torque made by the main rotor.

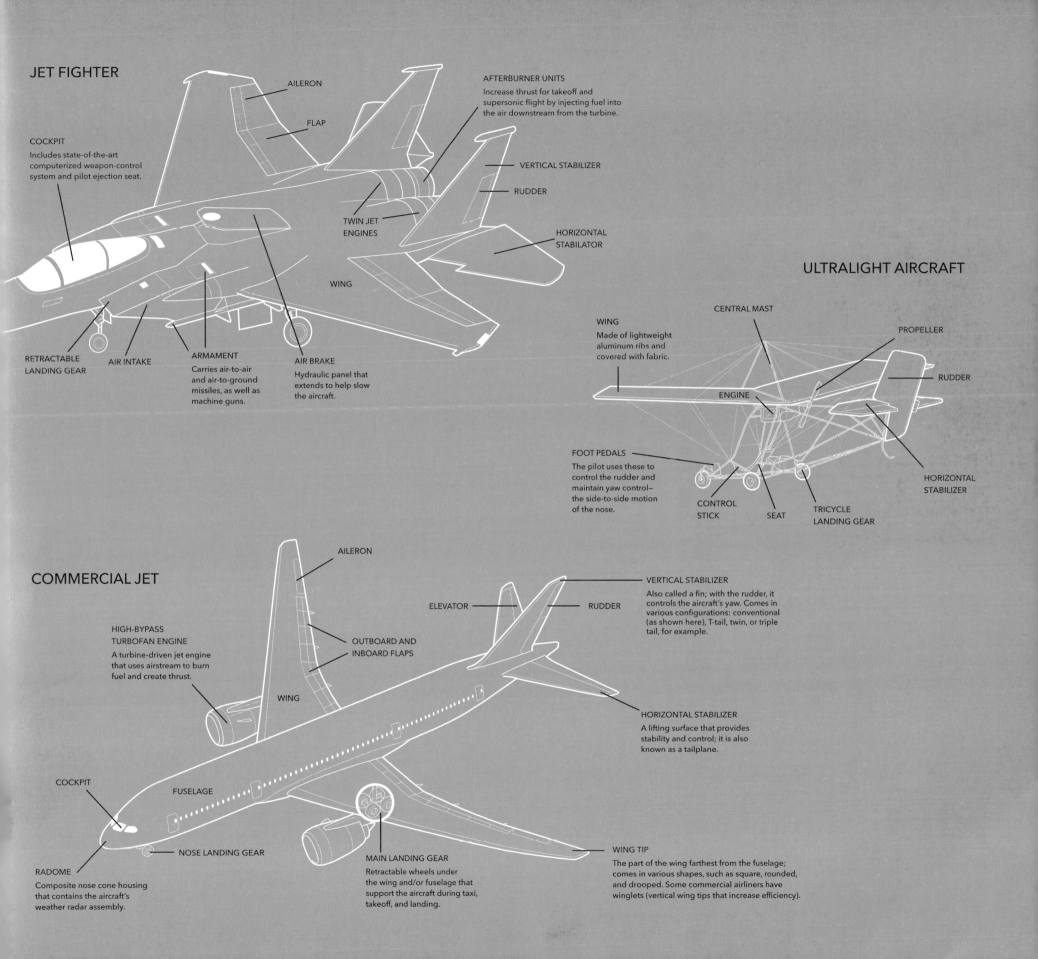

JET FIGHTER

AILERON

FLAP

AFTERBURNER UNITS
Increase thrust for takeoff and supersonic flight by injecting fuel into the air downstream from the turbine.

COCKPIT
Includes state-of-the-art computerized weapon-control system and pilot ejection seat.

VERTICAL STABILIZER

RUDDER

TWIN JET ENGINES

HORIZONTAL STABILATOR

WING

RETRACTABLE LANDING GEAR

AIR INTAKE

ARMAMENT
Carries air-to-air and air-to-ground missiles, as well as machine guns.

AIR BRAKE
Hydraulic panel that extends to help slow the aircraft.

ULTRALIGHT AIRCRAFT

WING
Made of lightweight aluminum ribs and covered with fabric.

CENTRAL MAST

PROPELLER

RUDDER

ENGINE

HORIZONTAL STABILIZER

FOOT PEDALS
The pilot uses these to control the rudder and maintain yaw control—the side-to-side motion of the nose.

CONTROL STICK

SEAT

TRICYCLE LANDING GEAR

COMMERCIAL JET

AILERON

VERTICAL STABILIZER
Also called a fin; with the rudder, it controls the aircraft's yaw. Comes in various configurations: conventional (as shown here), T-tail, twin, or triple tail, for example.

ELEVATOR

RUDDER

HIGH-BYPASS TURBOFAN ENGINE
A turbine-driven jet engine that uses airstream to burn fuel and create thrust.

OUTBOARD AND INBOARD FLAPS

WING

HORIZONTAL STABILIZER
A lifting surface that provides stability and control; it is also known as a tailplane.

COCKPIT

FUSELAGE

NOSE LANDING GEAR

MAIN LANDING GEAR
Retractable wheels under the wing and/or fuselage that support the aircraft during taxi, takeoff, and landing.

WING TIP
The part of the wing farthest from the fuselage; comes in various shapes, such as square, rounded, and drooped. Some commercial airliners have winglets (vertical wing tips that increase efficiency).

RADOME
Composite nose cone housing that contains the aircraft's weather radar assembly.

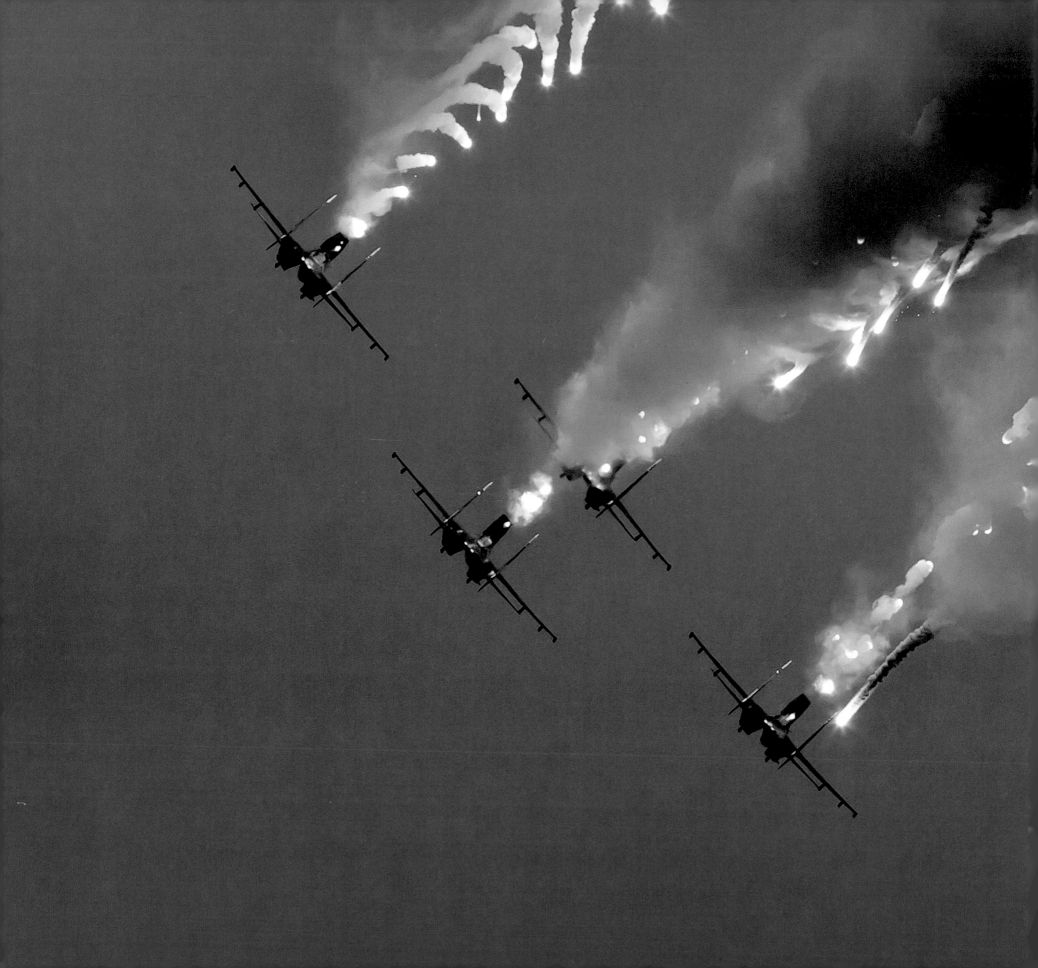

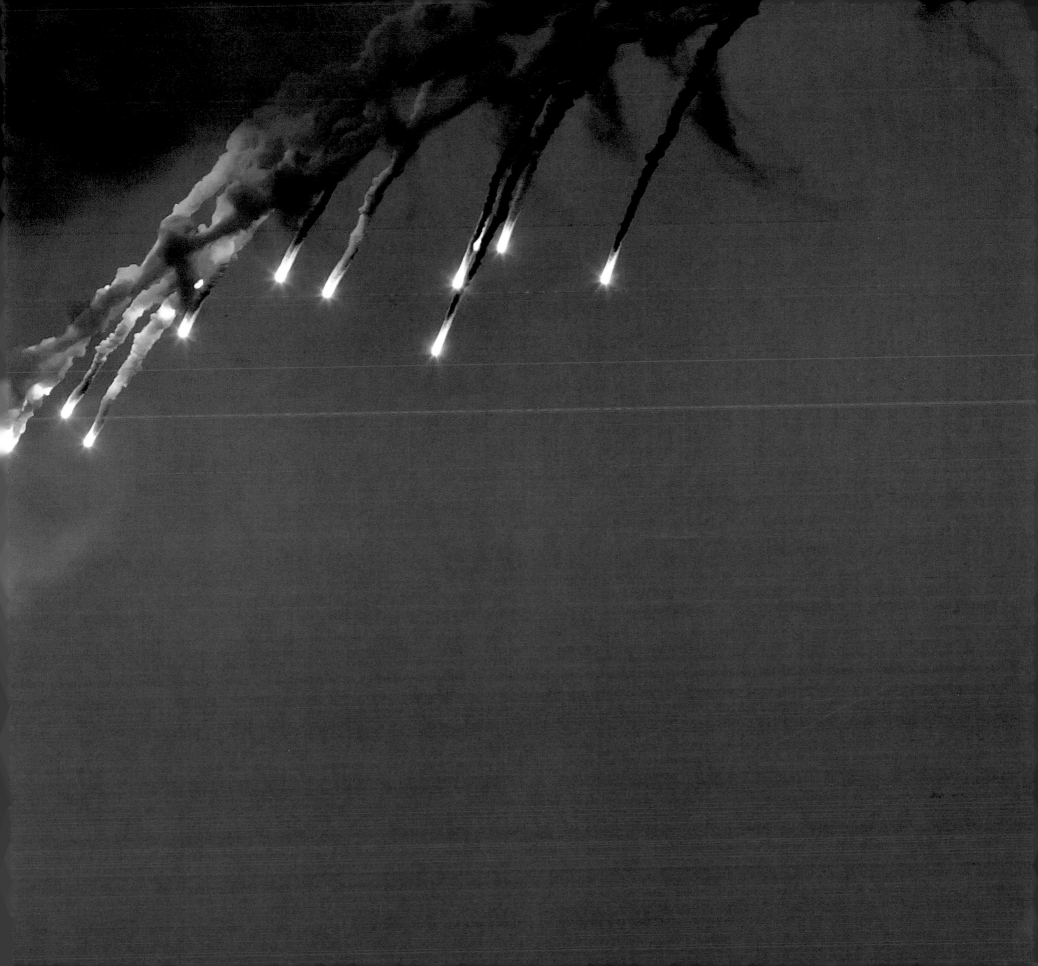

WRIGHT FLYER

The original *Wright Flyer* made history on the gusty morning of December 17, 1903, at Kill Devil Hills in Kitty Hawk, North Carolina. The *Flyer* (sometimes called the *Flyer I* or the *1903 Flyer*) was launched into the air for a mere twelve seconds over a distance of just 120 feet (36.5 m) with Orville Wright at the controls. It was the first heavier-than-air powered, controlled flight, a feat that a number of pioneering individuals and teams had been feverishly chasing.

On the fourth and final flight of the day, Wilbur Wright piloted the *Flyer* on its longest flight by far, remaining airborne for fifty-nine seconds over a distance of 852 feet (259.75 m). After landing, the *Flyer* was unfortunately blown over by a wind gust and heavily damaged—and it never flew again. But, with those first few trips aloft, the Wright brothers had documented that sustained, controlled, powered flight was possible, and their place in history was ensured. Understanding the historic significance of their airplane, the Wrights crated up its crumpled pieces and shipped them home to Dayton, Ohio. Today, the repaired *Wright Flyer* hangs in the Smithsonian National Air and Space Museum in Washington, D.C.

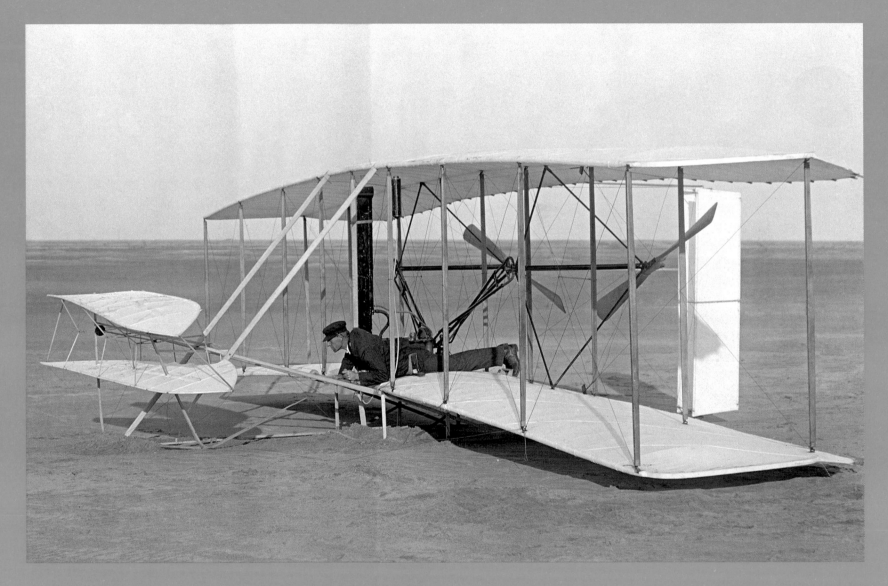

The *Wright Flyer* borrowed elements from the gliders that the Wright brothers had also successfully built and flown. To pilot the *Flyer*, for instance, Wilbur or Orville would lie on his stomach on the lower wing, strapped into a cradle that allowed him to steer with his hips.

DOUGLAS DC-3

It all started when Transcontinental and Western Airlines asked designer Donald Douglas to develop a two-engine airliner that could compete with United Airlines' modern, all-metal Boeing 247. The final result—the shiny aluminum DC-3—hit a sweet spot of performance and comfort that no other airplane had attained before. It first flew on December 17, 1935, and the first model was called the DST for "Douglas Sleeper Transport," seating up to twenty-four passengers, with room for sixteen overnight sleeping berths.

Even American Airlines saw the potential of this new airplane, and it ordered a fleet of DC-3s that would replace its Curtiss Condor biplanes. In 1941, 80 percent of commercial airliners in the United States were DC-3s, and the craft remained the most ubiquitous of airliners as late as 1948.

While the DC-3 came to epitomize the public's image of airline travel for decades following World War II, the airplane served multiple valuable roles in the military, too. A version of the Douglas painted in olive army drab was called the C-47. Still another, the R4D, was decked out in navy colors. Military pilots called the Douglas craft the Gooney Bird, and it distinguished itself in service in countless positions, including supplying troops "over the Hump" (beyond the Himalayan mountains) in Myanmar and delivering paratroopers to France in the wee morning hours of D-Day. General Dwight Eisenhower honored the aircraft by listing it as one of the four innovations that contributed most significantly to the Allies' World War II victory; the other three were the bazooka, the Jeep, and the atom bomb.

Donald Douglas's iconic DC-3 became the image of airline travel in the late 1930s, and close to 1,000 of the beauties are still in service almost eight decades later.

AIRBUS A380

The double-decker Airbus A380 rules as the largest airliner in the world. Airbus decided to take on the daunting project—competing with the Boeing 747's dominance among large airliners—based on the growing need to transport great numbers of people huge distances. No doubt, Airbus was counting on the assumption that the Asian economy would emerge as a major world force, stimulating the need for transportation among Asia, the United States, and Europe.

Its investment in the A380 has proved successful: Singapore Airlines, Emirates (Dubai, United Arab Emirates), Air France, Korean Air, China Southern Airlines, and others purchased and continue to operate the craft. And because the A380 is so big, many airports have had to upgrade their taxiways and ramps to accommodate

its unprecedented 261-foot (79.5-m) wingspan and exceptional weight. The double-decked, wide-bodied jet provides seating for 525 people in a typical three-class configuration or up to 853 people in all-economy class configurations. It can also carry a staggering 3,000 suitcases.

Original promotional drawings for the A380 included a piano lounge and a gym—but a version constructed without those extravagant additions made its maiden flight from Toulouse, France, where Airbus is based, in April 2005. The airplane's design incorporates advanced materials including carbon-fiber–reinforced plastics in the wings, fuselage sections, and tail, as well as highly capable avionics technology and four quiet and fuel-efficient turbofan engines.

Introduced in 2013, the Airbus A380-800 requires a massive runway. It must be at least 9,020 feet (2,750 m) in length and 200 feet (60 m) in width.

PIPER J-3 CUB

The airplane that taught a generation to fly—the distinctive bright yellow Piper J-3 Cub—is as instantly recognizable today as it was when it was first produced almost seventy-five years ago. During the Depression, only the wealthy could afford the high-powered Wacos, Stinsons, and Beechcraft cabin biplanes that dominated production. But the development of light, low-horsepower, and relatively cheap engines in the early 1930s made flight more accessible. Introduced in 1938, the J-3 Cub was an immediate hit due to its simplicity, affordability, and forgiving flying characteristics.

During World War II, the Cub donned olive drab, and the L-4 military version proved an excellent observation platform from which to spot enemy troop movements. Known as grasshoppers, Cubs also directed artillery, evacuated wounded soldiers, and served as multitasking aerial "Jeeps," capable of taking off from and landing on just about any short patch of clear ground.

At the height of production, a new Cub was rolling out of the factory in Lock Haven, Pennsylvania, at the surprising rate of one every twenty minutes. After the war, William T. Piper priced the Cub at U.S.$2,195—a sound investment for returning GIs who yearned to fly. It made a lasting impression: The term *Cub* is still used to describe any small high-wing airplane. All told, some 20,000 J-3 Cubs and L-4s were made before the end of production in 1947.

Piper Cubs—with their bright yellow paint, squat taildragger landing gear, and open clamshell doors—evoke a special nostalgia for many pilots. In addition to standard landing gear, they can be outfitted with skis or floats, as shown here.

BEECHCRAFT STARSHIP

The brainchild of legendary aircraft designer Burt Rutan, the Beechcraft Starship was a radical departure from conventional designs—Rutan started fresh with many untried concepts. The Starship was intended to kick-start the next generation of aircraft, picking up where Beech's exemplary King Air turboprop twin series left off. With twin-pusher turboprop engines, an all-glass cockpit, a canard configuration (in which small wings are positioned in front of the main wings), two vertical winglets instead of one main tail, and a carbon-fiber composite construction new to civilian aircraft, the Starship was ahead of its time when Beechcraft contracted with Rutan's Scaled Composites in 1981 to build an 85-percent-scale proof of concept.

It proved to be a long road toward certification, however. The combination of an unproven construction technique and a configuration that confounded certification officials led to mandates to overbuild the airframe, which added weight and robbed performance. In the end, the project culminated with the flight of the first production Starship in 1989. The airplane turned out to be a comfortable, quiet corporate transport, efficient and versatile.

Despite excellent performance—even with the weight penalty imposed by regulatory authorities—only fifty-three Starships were ever built. Beechcraft blamed slow sales of the model on a down economy, a costly complimentary maintenance program, and the airplane's unconventional looks, reinforcing the traditional maxim that, in business aviation, "funny-looking airplanes" don't sell. In 2003, Beech began buying back Starships, and many of them have been decommissioned and destroyed. Only five privately owned Starships exist today.

The 1980s Beechcraft Starship was a wonder of modern design. Built with composites and featuring a forward-wing canard configuration, the short-lived Starship was ahead of its time and outside most buyers' comfort zones.

YAKOVLEV YAK-9

Produced by the thousands in the mid-1940s, the Yak-9 was one of Russia's most notorious World War II fighters and one of its best performers. Like the British Spitfire and the American P-51 Mustang, the Yak-9 was powered by V-12 liquid-cooled engines, including the Soviet-produced Klimov M-107 engine, among others.

Designed by Alexander Sergeyevich Yakovlev, the Yak-9 was produced in more than twenty different versions, with its production lasting from 1942 to 1948. In fact, the Yak-9 would become one of the most modified aircraft designs of the war, arriving at the front at various times with two different wing designs, five different engines, six fuel tank configurations, and seven varying combinations of armament. Its striking airframe was constructed of metal and then covered with a skin made of Bakelite, one of the first synthetic plastics.

Even though its M-107 engine suffered from oil leaks and coolant problems, the Yak-9 was successful enough that German Luftwaffe pilots were at one point told not to risk engaging in combat with them. The aircraft was also used by North Korea against the Allies in the Korean War. Its winning points were excellent maneuverability and speeds of greater than 400 miles per hour (643.75 km/h) in versions equipped with the 1,650-horsepower Kilmov VK-107A engine variant. The plane's downsides, like many fighters of its time, were poor engine reliability and the inability to carry large amounts of armament.

Sometimes mistaken for a Mustang or a Spitfire, the Russian Yak-9 shared their V-12 in-line engine configuration and general layout.

At U.S.$12,750 in 1947, the price tag on the 195 was a bit steep, and Cessna called it the BusinessLiner to increase its profile among the well-to-do executive set. Its larger cabin and classy good looks helped seal the deal.

CESSNA 195

The vast majority of Cessna's piston-engine planes are known as tame, reliable family fliers: Most have wings stabilized with struts and cabins built with man-size pilots in mind. But back in the day, Clyde Cessna was known for building fast airplanes. His racers from the 1930s featured low, sleek fuselages and sported among the first cantilevered wings, meaning that all the support structure was inside, with no need for draggy external struts of wires. The Cessna 190/195 series came along between the 1930s racers and the mostly slower and more utilitarian models of the 1950s.

Introduced to the public just after World War II in 1947 (the same year as Beech's Bonanza), the airplane sported a cowl that surrounded the 195's round engine and flowed backward to a sleek, cigar-shaped fuselage. The five-seat cabin was roomy and sat beneath one of Cessna's signature high wings. It was fast and efficient, a good competitor to Beech's prewar radial-engine Staggerwing. But the 195's tail-wheel landing-gear configuration, which was conventional at the time, was tricky for novice pilots.

Cessna tried to solve the latter problem with a unique landing-gear apparatus that pivoted with the wind, but it didn't work the way its designers had hoped. Though Cessna shut down production in 1954, today's owners of 195s cherish them for their art deco look, that great radial-engine sound, and classic big-cabin comfort.

ERCOUPE

Fred Weick's little side-by-side flier was a revolutionary approach to personal aviation. He designed the Ercoupe in the mid-1930s to be so safe that just about anyone could fly one. The name combined his company's acronym, Engineering Research Co., or ERCO, with the common name for a two-seat car, coupe. Weick's research into stall-proof, spin-proof aerodynamics began when he worked for the National Advisory Committee on Aeronautics (later to become NASA). He left NACA in 1936 and joined ERCO.

The snappy twin-tail Ercoupe was an 85-mile-per-hour (136.75-km/h) cruiser and featured many modern design approaches, including metal construction, excellent visibility through a greenhouse canopy, and tricycle landing gear. The Ercoupe also boasted two-axis, rudderless, stall-proof aerodynamics. The elevator control, which adjusts the airplane's pitch up or down, was limited, making it nearly impossible for the pilot to stall. It also had interconnected controls blending inputs to the ailerons and rudder, so there were no rudder pedals for the pilot to manipulate.

But for all of its safety advances, pilots managed to find ways to crash it anyway: The Ercoupe's safety record was ultimately no better than those of its contemporaries. The design bounced around for decades among numerous manufacturers, including Mooney Aircraft, which gave it a single tail and reintroduced rudder control for the pilot. Today, the Ercoupe is much loved by its hundreds of owners for being a stable, two-seat, fun little flier, just as Weick envisioned.

The Ercoupe was sometimes nicknamed the "poor man's P-38"—a reference to its twin tails, which slightly resemble the twin-boom configuration of the Lockheed P-38 Lightning.

BOEING 314 CLIPPER

In the 1930s, the concept of world air travel was just taking hold. Surmising that traveling by air was an extension of traveling by ocean liner, Pan American Airways (Pan Am) adopted the flying boat concept. The theory was that most international destinations might not have a runway, but more than likely, they would have an open stretch of nearby water. The resulting massive flying boats were dubbed "Clippers" after the exemplary sailing ships. Designed and built for Pan Am in the late 1930s and early '40s, the Boeing 314 Clipper ushered in the era of transoceanic passenger flight.

Built using the wings and nacelle—the cover around engine and fuel equipment—of Boeing's existing XB-15 bomber prototype, the Clipper's four 1,500-horsepower Wright Double Cyclone engines gave the 84,000-pound (38-mt) flying boat the muscle needed to cross an ocean. Only a dozen were built between 1938 and 1941, when World War II put an end to the romance of the Clippers. With room for ten crew members and seventy-four passengers, the Boeing 314 treated those aboard to spacious dining and sleeping quarters as well as gourmet meals catered by four-star hotels for a luxurious experience in the air.

The era of the Pan Am Clippers was a short but iconic chapter in aviation history. After World War II, these beautiful flying boats were replaced by airliners with longer ranges that didn't require the robust training programs and large crews of the Clippers.

PITTS SPECIAL

With a silhouette so compact it looks as if it could be hung from a rearview mirror, the tiny Pitts Special biplane was not designed for stability—but its short wings and relatively large rudder make it an excellent aerobatic airplane. Curtis Pitts was way ahead of his time when he designed this airplane in the mid-1940s: With four ailerons to help control the plane, the Pitts has a bumblebee-fast roll rate (the degrees per second by which an airplane can shift from side to side). Its steel-tube fuselage and strutted wings with interlaced flying wires make the airplane nearly indestructible. When it first appeared, its control, harmony, and balance made it the aerobatic performer against which all others were judged.

Pitts's own hand-drawn plans had to suffice for home-plane builders who wanted their own until about 1966, when professional plans were drawn up.

Thereafter, Pitts began working on a two-seat trainer version to be known as the S2, and the original became the S1. Aerobatic performer Betty Skelton made the airplane famous, darting and rolling through competitions in *Little Stinker*, the second Pitts S1 single-seat airplane built by Curtis Pitts. Her airplane is now on display at the Smithsonian National Air and Space Museum in Washington, D.C.

Legendary air-show pilot Bob Herendeen flew a Pitts S1 for the U.S. Aerobatic Team at the World Aerobatic competition in Moscow in 1966. In 1972, the U.S. Aerobatic Team won the world championship—and by then all team members were flying Pitts. The Pitts Special is still widely used in air shows today, and the S1 and its two-seat brother, the S2, are still produced by Aviat Aircraft in Afton, Wyoming.

Pitts Specials are spectacular when flying in formation. The Trig Aerobatic Team, a civilian air-show team that flies Pitts Special S-1Ds, still performs in air shows all over Europe.

AERODYNAMIC ADVANCES

For centuries, we've sought answers to the secret of flight by watching the birds and contemplating the movements of their sleek, aerodynamic bodies. The quest to emulate feathered flight has led humans down many conceptual paths—some more successful than others. In the end, the study of air and wing opened up the skies to exploration, and refining that study continues to this day and beyond.

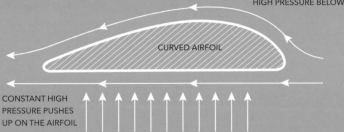

LOW AIR PRESSURE ABOVE THE AIRFOIL, LIFTED BY THE HIGH PRESSURE BELOW

CURVED AIRFOIL

CONSTANT HIGH PRESSURE PUSHES UP ON THE AIRFOIL

1905

Ailerons – Glenn Curtiss

The Wright brothers discovered that warping an airplane's wings controlled bank angle, and they patented their system. Glenn Curtiss's airplanes used a better idea: small movable wings on each side of the airplane called "ailerons" fitted on the ends of the main wings. By moving one up and the other down, he achieved the same effect as warping the main wings, only much more efficiently.

1926–1931

Quantum Leaps – Schneider Trophy Racers

Through the late 1920s and early 1930s, the Schneider Trophy races pitted nation against nation in a quest to design the fastest seaplanes. The results were rapid-fire, state-of-the-art advancements in both aerodynamics and engine design, with extreme streamlining and tightly cowled, inline, liquid-cooled engines. The 1931 winner, the British Supermarine S6.B (which would inspire the WWII Spitfire fighter) was the first to break the 400-mile-per-hour (643.75-km/h) barrier, clocking in at 407.5 miles per hour (655.75 km/h).

1738

Going with the Flow – Bernoulli's Principle

Swiss scientist Daniel Bernoulli published what has become known as Bernoulli's Principle in 1738. Its tenets suggest that air will reduce in pressure when forced over the top of a curved airfoil. Because the pressure of the air passing below the surface remains constant, lowering pressure on top leads to lift. Bernoulli never saw an airplane, but his findings have nevertheless sparked a perpetual debate among pilots regarding what really makes a wing fly.

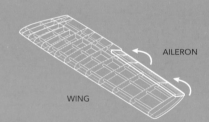

AILERON

WING

1900

Wing Warping – Wright Brothers

Wilbur and Orville first opened their eyes to the possibilities of manned flight by studying how kites flew and how they could control them. One day, holding an empty cardboard box that had contained a bicycle inner tube, Wilbur twisted it back and forth, discovering the concept of "wing warping," or controlling a wing's shape and increasing its lift on one side while decreasing its lift on the other. Thus, he unlocked the secret of controlling an airplane's roll axis.

1909

Rearranging the Airplane's Controls – Louis Blériot

Inspired by other aviation researchers in Europe, financially well-off French inventor Louis Blériot devoted his energy to refining the airplane. When he crashed his Blériot V monoplane on takeoff, perhaps he realized he was lucky not to have been crushed by its aft-mounted engine. His follow-on designs placed the engine and propeller in the nose, with the elevator and rudder offset to the rear. The Blériot XI got him across the English Channel with what became the standard aerodynamic configuration.

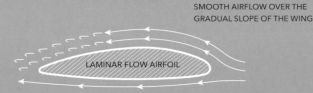

SMOOTH AIRFLOW OVER THE
GRADUAL SLOPE OF THE WING

LAMINAR FLOW AIRFOIL

INTERRUPTED AIRFLOW OVER
DRASTIC SLOPE OF THE WING

CONVENTIONAL AIRFOIL

CIGAR-SHAPED
FUSELAGE

WASP-WAISTED
FUSELAGE

1942

Laminar Flow – North American Aviation

In developing the P-51 Mustang, designers at North American Aviation had an ace up their sleeves that they were itching to put into play. Using wind-tunnel research on laminar-flow wing design borrowed from the National Advisory Committee for Aeronautics, they changed the traditional shape of the wing so it was wider at the center, making air pass over its gradual slope in a smooth manner and maximizing efficiency at high speed. The Mustang's wing is fattest at around two-thirds of the way between the leading and trailing edges—much farther aft than any before. This allowed the airflow to stick to the surface far longer at high speed, resulting in lower drag. Its laminar-flow wing was among the biggest reasons the Mustang became one of history's greatest fighters.

1959

Area Rule – Richard T. Whitcomb

Research around World War II revealed that airflow around an airplane would accelerate, and as it approached the speed of sound, some areas of the airframe would experience supersonic airflow—resulting in irregular buffeting and other disadvantages. So designers adjusted the shape of fast jets' fuselages, giving them a wasp-waisted look, also known as the coke-bottle shape. The so-called area-rule effect culminated in Richard T. Whitcomb's design of the Convair F-106 Delta Dart.

1976

Supersonic for Civilians – Concorde

It was close to three decades after the Bell X-1 first broke the sound barrier that a supersonic civilian airliner went into service. The Anglo-French Concorde cruised at Mach 2.04 and featured four massive Rolls-Royce/Snecma engines to power its dizzying speed, a signature double-delta wing configuration that prevented shock waves at supersonic speeds, and massive intake ramps that slowed incoming air to Mach 0.5, preventing engine-damaging shocks.

1947

Breaking Mach 1 – Bell Aircraft Company

The speed of sound—Mach 1—was a major barrier aircraft designers faced in the quest to go higher, farther, and faster. Approaching that magic speed led to wild buffeting, flutter, and other aerodynamic challenges. The Bell X-1 borrowed its basic shape from an object designers knew could achieve Mach 1: a .50 caliber bullet. With that, Chuck Yeager was able to successfully break the sound barrier in his Bell X-1 *Glamorous Glennis* (named for his wife) on October 14, 1947.

1949

Swept Wing – MiG 15

Supersonic flight had been achieved, but planes traveling at such immense speed encountered a problem: Changing air pressures at Mach 1 caused shock waves to form on the wing, resulting in drag. To counter this trouble, the Germans started experimenting with swept wings, which reduce curvature in the airflow and greatly increase speeds. But the Russians—who captured the German data after World War II—were the first to translate theory into a successful design: the feared MiG-15 fighter, with its wings slanted from root to tip at a 35-degree angle. The swept wing is now de rigueur on all supersonic and fighter jets.

WING ROOT

35-DEGREE ANGLE

WING TIP

2012

Mach-Teasing Business Jet – Gulfstream G650

Gulfstream's latest jet, the G650, can fly at Mach .925, but that's only part of the story. Its advanced wing design and fly-by-wire computerized controls also give the business jet twenty-first–century performance at the low end of the speed range, allowing remarkably short takeoff and landing for such a capable, wide-cabin jet. The computerized controls also smooth out the ride, continually readjusting the control surfaces for turbulent conditions. With a range of 7,000 nautical miles (12,964 km), a full kitchen, and berthing sleeper seats, the U.S.$65 million G650 is the ultimate in worldwide executive transportation.

CESSNA CITATION I

The Citation 500 launched Cessna's hugely successful business jet line, which today spans a whole family of airplanes based on the original type certificate as well as follow-on, reimagined models. FAA-certified in 1971, the original turbofan-powered Citation 500 was immediately snubbed by the aviation press for being 120 knots slower than the turbojet-powered Learjet 25, earning it the nicknames Slowtation and Nearjet. But Cessna had the last laugh: Undeterred, the Wichita, Kansas, manufacturer improved the model with a longer wingspan, increased gross weight, and thrust reversers that allowed operations from shorter runways. The rechristened and undeniably successful jet was named the Citation I.

With an eye toward widening its market to owner-pilots, Cessna improved the model yet again with the Citation I/SP, a new version that could be operated by a single pilot (rather than the two pilots needed at the helm of the original Citation I). It became an instant hit. That spirit lives on with Cessna's current CitationJet series and the Citation Mustang light jet, designed with the owner-pilot operator in mind.

A testament to the community of Citation owners is the Special Olympics Airlift, a Cessna-organized operation in which volunteer owners and their crews fly Special Olympics athletes from all over the country to take part in national competitions, returning them home after the closing ceremonies. Today, decades after the first Citation was introduced and almost twenty years after the last Citation I rolled off the assembly line, nobody would dare ridicule the Cessna Citation line, which has earned a coveted place as one of the best-selling and most-loved business jets of all time.

The Cessna Citation I was one of the first members of the corporate jet class to be powered by turbofan engines, giving it greater efficiency and range than its earlier turbojet competitors, such as the first Lear Jets.

BOEING B-17 FLYING FORTRESS

A beloved American icon, the Boeing B-17 Flying Fortress remains one of the most celebrated warbirds in U.S. history. From its menacing twin tail guns to its polished Plexiglas nose, the B-17 was a blend of reliable performance and rugged beauty that packed up to thirteen machine guns and an 8,000-pound (3.75-mt) bomb payload. The airplane's computerized Norden bombsight—its bomb-aiming device—was so top secret that bombardiers were instructed to remove it after flight, cover it with their jackets in photographs, and destroy it in the event of a forced landing in enemy territory.

The Flying Fortress design borrowed from both the experimental Boeing XB-15 and the Model 247 airliner. Launched in the 1930s, the craft was a vital component of the Allied offensive in Europe: B-17s dropped more than half a million tons (453,592 mt) of bombs on Germany during World War II, earning them both a widespread reputation for their ability to withstand severe combat damage and their nickname. Its charisma and fame in battle also landed it on the big screen: The wartime documentary *Memphis Belle* focused on a B-17 that survived to complete a whopping twenty-five missions. Another film, *12 O'Clock High*, imagined life on a base in England. And in real life, Clark Gable served as a B-17 crewman and Jimmy Stewart as a pilot, though he flew B-24s.

Of the 12,731 B-17s built between 1936 and 1945, about a dozen remain airworthy today. Several more are under restoration, including the actual *Memphis Belle*. Many more of the classic aircraft can be viewed around the United States.

The *Memphis Belle*—a B-17 named for Margaret Polk, the girlfriend of pilot Lt. Robert Morgan—features custom nose art based on a pinup image from *Esquire* magazine.

BENSEN B-8
GYROCOPTER

Gyrocopters (also called autogyros or autogiros) predate helicopters. The basic principles of rotary-wing lift and control are the same for both types of aircraft, but while a helicopter's rotors are powered, a gyrocopter's rotors are not. They spin like a pinwheel as they pass through the air, much like an oak tree's seed pod. A gyrocopter cannot hover, and it needs a short runway to get airborne, but it can achieve a safe landing in a clear space the size of a tennis court. To launch, a gyrocopter needs forward thrust, which can come from either being towed behind a car or boat, or from an engine with a propeller attached.

During World War II, German submarines towed and sent up Focke-Achgelis Fa 330 gyrocopters to look for Allied convoys, then reeled them in, folded their rotors, and stowed them to submerge and attack. In the 1950s Russian immigrant Igor Bensen converted that concept into a powered gyrocopter. Using a small surplus McCulloch engine to drive a pusher propeller, the Bensen Gyrocopter kit was inexpensive, decidedly low-tech, and easy to build. The pilot sat up front in the open air, with the engine and propeller behind and the spinning rotor above. As with a helicopter, the controls altered the pitch of the rotor blades at varying segments of its arc, raising or lowering the nose and banking left or right. It had a large rudder for control. Bensen's creation was incredibly fun to fly and, consequently, an instant sales success. Bensen delivered thousands of kits and plans throughout more than three decades. Today, gyrocopters remain a niche segment of sport flying.

Shown here, the B-8M is a motorized variant of the beloved B-8. In 1966, Igor Bensen himself replicated the Wright brothers' first flight in a B-8M, which he dubbed *The Spirit of Kitty Hawk*.

CANADAIR CRJ

Canadair (now Bombardier) pioneered the concept of the regional jet airliner with its RJ series. Based on Canadair's impressive Challenger business jet, the first RJs were met with skepticism: Experts wondered how a big jet could possibly be economically feasible on short routes, since large jets traditionally flew at high altitudes to enable efficient fuel burn. Turboprops had always been the go-to aircraft for short runs flown at lower altitude. The flying public, on the other hand, was amenable to jets: If an airplane had propellers, they assumed it used outdated technology. Thus, with new and more efficient fan engines, the stage was set for the positive reception of the RJ, a short-distance jet.

The first RJs were a rousing success on short routes. Its business-jet heritage from the Challenger line is evident when looking at its pointy nose and wide fuselage. With several variants offering seating for between forty and one-hundred passengers, the CRJ line quickly became a favorite among regional airlines around the world after its introduction in 1992.

The twin-engine jet design enabled not only quick and economical short hops but also cost-efficient midrange flights. Such flights had previously been serviced only by heavier aircraft, such as the Boeing 737, which often flew those routes with many empty seats. Airlines also liked the lower salaries paid to regional jet pilots. Just one complication arose: Pilots' unions protested the use of RJs on the midrange routes previously flown by larger jets with higher-paid crews. But that hasn't stop more than 1,600 CRJs from being delivered to date. Today, the CRJ1000 variant seats as many as one hundred passengers.

For the CRJ, Canadair took the standard Challenger cabin cross section, stretched it by nearly 20 feet (6 m) in length to fit more passengers, and installed airline-style seating, with two seats on each side of the aisle.

LOCKHEED MARTIN F-22 RAPTOR

Since the F-22 emerged in 2005, the fifth-generation fighter has displayed a winning combination of cutting-edge stealth technology, supersonic cruise capability, and superb air-combat maneuverability—all unmatched by any fighter in the world. Its place at the top remains unchallenged: Fifth-generation combat adversaries from rival Russian and Chinese design bureaus have not lived up to expectations, leaving the F-22 without a worthy foe to engage. Even so, a ban on exports has led for calls to cease production of the Raptor in favor of the less expensive and more versatile multirole F-35 Lightning II.

But those economic concerns don't make the Raptor any less impressive: Powered by two Pratt & Whitney F119 engines that deliver 35,000 pounds (16 mt) of thrust each, the single-pilot F-22 is able to reach speeds beyond Mach 2.0 with the use of afterburners (an engine feature that increases thrust) and speeds above Mach 1.5 without them. The aircraft's stealth technology gives it a radar signature the size of a steel marble, while the jet's sensor fusion offers its pilots better situational awareness than ever. It's also the only fighter jet that can engage in both air-to-air and air-to-ground combat missions at the same time, establishing it as a double threat all over the world.

Despite the Raptor's operational glitches and notoriously high development costs, the jet is still considered the most advanced tactical fighter on the planet.

Captured here in a low-level, high-G turn, the ever-stealthy F-22 Raptor's distinctive wing shape makes equally distinctive and diminutive condensation trails. Even the exhaust plume is muted to create as low an infrared signature as possible.

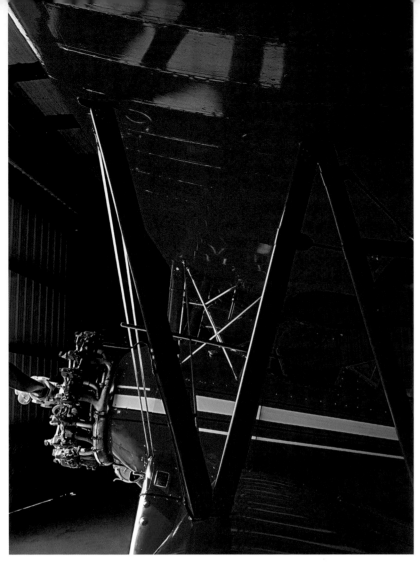

BOEING-STEARMAN PT-17 BIPLANE

Most U.S. army pilots of World War II learned to fly in a PT-17. Though the war ended long ago, the fascination with this charming model hasn't waned. A rugged biplane with wooden wing spars, a steel-tube fuselage, and fabric covering, the Stearman had a pair of massive wings mated to each other by a network of struts and bracing wires. Student cadets in their open-front cockpits learned to judge speed by the sound of the wind whistling through the flying wires. That is, of course, when that sound wasn't muffled by instructors shouting from the back seat through an "intercom," which was just a rubber tube running from the instructor's speaking port to the student's cloth flying helmet.

The Stearman is one of the planes most beloved by restorers and collectors. Its creator, Lloyd Stearman (who went on to become president of Lockheed Aircraft Company), likely had no idea that his name would someday become synonymous with the word *biplane,* or that his design would train the world's best military pilots. Its responsive flight controls, forgiving performance, and dependable 220-horsepower Continental R-670 engine contributed to the Stearman's status as the ideal military trainer. After its military heyday passed, the biplane saw new life as a crop duster, sport plane, and air-show craft. Boeing bought Stearman's design and produced 9,800, ending its run in 1945.

The Piper PA-46 Malibu series includes the sole in-production example of a pressurized owner-flown airplane with a single-piston engine: the Malibu Mirage. The line started in the early 1980s with the Malibu, a cruiser with speeds around 230 miles per hour (370 km/h). It had a comfortable club-seating cabin in back and could fly as high as 25,000 feet (7,620 m) with a range of 1,789 miles (2,879 km). These features made the airplane very attractive to buyers with long-range missions who wanted to fly above the weather.

In the late '80s, the Malibu got a new, more powerful Lycoming engine due to initial problems with the original Continental engine. This caused the plane to decrease somewhat in range capability, but the Malibu Mirage continues to be a good seller for Piper. Next, Piper upped the ante further with the Malibu Meridian, a turboprop derivative powered by the reliable Pratt & Whitney Canada PT6A. The added reliability and power of the turboprop was a welcome upgrade for buyers.

Piper's next move caught a lot of industry observers by surprise. In 2007, Piper introduced the Malibu Matrix, which appeared to be a downgrade because it was a nonpressurized version of the piston-powered Mirage. But, as it turns out, with recession looming, Piper got it right with the Matrix. By eliminating pressurization, the Matrix lost some of its high-altitude capability, but it costs almost U.S.$200,000 less than the Mirage. It still retains the comfortable cabin-class seating for passengers and is targeted as a step-up for owners of smaller high-performance aircraft such as the Cirrus SR22.

The Malibu Mirage, shown here, featured all the comfort and range of the original Malibu, but it contained a more reliable engine.

DIAMOND DA40

Born of European composite sailplane technology, Diamond Aircraft's four-seat Diamond DA40 has a slick, rivet-free fuselage, and it easily outruns and outclimbs a new Cessna 172, despite having the same fuel-efficient, four-cylinder engine. Add modern glass-panel avionics, and the four-seat DA40 has all the hallmarks of a successful cruiser.

Diamond was one of the first to embrace computerized avionics in the form of Garmin's impressive G1000 panel. It includes large-screen moving maps, onboard weather information, synthetic vision (for a computerized view of the real-world terrain below), and traffic alerts. With safety in mind, the Diamond DA40's long wings give it nice gliding ability—a benefit in the case of engine failure but also a measure of the design's efficiency. But there is a trade-off: Low wing loading makes for a rougher ride in turbulence.

Some positive factors come into play due to the Diamond being designed so close to the twenty-first century. Its seats can withstand a 26 G-force impact, contributing to an exceptional safety record. With its good manners in flight and visibility from the cockpit greenhouse that rivals the scene on an IMAX screen, the Diamond tempts pilots looking for the latest in light-airplane technology.

The efficiency of the Diamond DA40's long wings, sleek composite airframe, and tricycle landing gear give it a jaunty look.

SUPERMARINE SPITFIRE

Proudly remembered as the aircraft that helped save the United Kingdom during the Battle of Britain in 1940, the Supermarine Spitfire has gained iconic status as one of the most famous fighters of all time. The aircraft's signature drag-reducing elliptical wings and sleek aerodynamic design gave it exceptional speed and maneuverability, which, combined with the fighter's eight machine guns, made the Spitfire a formidable foe. Powered by the almost equally famous Rolls-Royce Merlin V-12 engine, Spitfires were also well mannered to fly, without any dangerous quirks.

Its relative ease of use was a good thing: Many of its pilots were teenagers rushed through training when England's need was the greatest. Some were flying their first combat missions with less than six hours of Spitfire experience. Others were bomber or transport pilots pressed into service in Spitfires. The Spitfire was designed with all this in mind by Supermarine genius R. J. Mitchell, a young engineer who cut his teeth on the Schneider Cup racers of the 1920s.

Though stricken with cancer, Mitchell worked on the Spitfire as long as he possibly could, well understanding how deeply the country needed it. He got to see the prototype fly but did not live to see the airplane enter service with the Royal Air Force. First introduced in 1938, the Spitfire was continually improved and upgraded throughout the war. The fighter went on to become the most-produced British aircraft of World War II and it eventually served the country and its Allies in numbers greater than 20,000.

The Supermarine Spitfire was crucial to Britain's defense during World War II. Here, two Spitfires sport Royal Air Force roundels reserved for fighters in the 1940s.

AH-64 APACHE

In the early 1970s, the U.S. Army was looking for a replacement for the Bell Huey-Cobra, the gun-equipped variant of the Vietnam era's quintessential transport helicopter. Hughes Helicopters won the competition with its Model 77 advanced attack helicopter proposal, and the Apache was born. It made its first flight in September 1975 and entered service with the army in April 1986 as the AH-64. With its squared-off lines and aggressive stance, the Apache is one of the most predatory-looking aircraft ever. More than 1,200 have been built by Hughes, McDonnell Douglas, and Boeing, as the corporate entities shifted and overlapped over the years.

Powered by a pair of General Electric T700-series turboshaft engines producing up to 2,000 horsepower apiece, the U.S.$20 million Apache is equipped with a sophisticated nose-mounted sensor suite including forward-looking infrared night-vision components. A 30-mm chain gun rides under the belly between the landing gear, and there are four external points located under the stub wings that carry missiles and rockets. Pilots sit in a tandem fuselage that's narrow, making it hard to hit and easy to transport, and the four-blade main and tail rotors are remarkably damage tolerant.

Apaches were deployed during Operation Desert Storm in January 1991, and eight AH-64s conducted the first aerial operation of the conflict, demolishing the Iraqi radar network. In all, 277 Apaches took part in the war, destroying more than 500 enemy tanks. One was lost to a rocket-propelled grenade fired at close range, but the crew survived.

Often, the Apache would use its optical sensors to serve as the target identifier, and then fast jets would conduct the attack, allowing the helicopter to preserve its ammunition.

TBM 700/800/850

Civilian single-engine turboprops are fast, reliable, and easy to fly compared with other airplanes, including most piston-engine planes and twin turboprops. So when the French company Socata teamed up with Mooney Aircraft after it and its cabin-class, pressurized single-piston airplane had fallen into the fiscal doldrums, they ramped up their line to include the first successful civilian pressurized, single-engine turboprop. The TBM 700 resulted.

The TBM 700 was powered by a Pratt & Whitney PT6A-64 engine rated at 700 shaft horsepower. Subsequent models upgraded to more powerful engines, culminating in the TBM 850's P&W PT6A-66 with 850 horsepower.

One market advantage of the TBMs is the ability of potential customers to obtain insurance: It's significantly easier and less expensive to get the blessing of an underwriter when there is only one turboprop in the front of an airplane. Thus the TBM—as well as other planes that feature the reliable PT6A engine, such as certain Bonanzas and Cessnas—enjoys near-jet speeds with the simplicity of a propeller-driven single engine. Another benefit of operating a unique turboprop single such as the TBM is an active support network of fellow owner-pilots. The TBM owners group even publishes its own magazine chronicling TBM-related information and adventures.

One of the world's fastest single-engine turboprops, the TBM 850 can climb to 31,000 feet (9,448.75 m) in just under twenty minutes. Those along for the ride enjoy a comfortable, luxury experience in its sleek and luxurious cabin.

NORTH AMERICAN F-86 SABRE

Introduced by the makers of the popular P-51 Mustang, the swept-wing North American F-86 Sabre was designed using principles gleaned from German aerodynamic research that was obtained at the end of World War II. The Germans had discovered that swept wings performed better near the speed of sound, and the Russians had intercepted that intel—which explained why swept-wing Russian MiG-15s fared so well against earlier-generation straight-wing Lockheed F-80s and Republic F-84s when they first faced the Allies over Korea. When the swept-wing Sabres arrived on the scene, a tough matchup ensued, but the MiGs continued to outperform early Sabres in speed and climb.

Later-model Sabres were said to have the edge over the MiGs with regard to maneuverability, though, and the American fighters' six .50-caliber machine guns proved superior to the cannon-equipped MiGs due to the guns' faster rate of fire and greater muzzle velocity. Though the MiGs' cannon shells did more damage when they found their mark, it was tougher to lay a glove on the Sabres during high-speed jet-against-jet aerial war.

Recent research challenges the oft-quoted 10:1 victory ratio over Russian MiG-15s in the Korean War, revising that figure down to closer to 2:1. Even so, since its entry into service in 1951, the F-86 and its many variants have proven their versatility as high-altitude fighters, fighter-bombers, and all-weather interceptors. All in all, close to 10,000 F-86s were produced, with the fast-flying aircraft serving not only the United States and Canada, but also the forces of twenty other nations.

The F-86 Sabre set a world speed record of 670 miles per hour (1,078.25 km/h) in 1948, and it held the title until 1952.

ALBATROS D-SERIES

The Albatros D-series was a family of models built by German company Albatros-Flugzeugwerke to serve as fighters in World War I. Introduced in 1916, the Albatros was powered by a six-cylinder, liquid-cooled Mercedes engine ranging from 150 to 185 horsepower. These biplanes featured semi-monocoque fuselages, meaning that the fuselage structure was supported by its external skin, allowing minimal internal structure. This construction technique made the airplanes lighter and more aerodynamic than their fabric-covered predecessors and was revolutionary at the time, presaging the all-metal semimonocoque designs that dominated World War II–vintage fighters. The

development also permitted the rounded fuselages that gave these airplanes a sleek and birdlike appearance, in stark contrast to some other fighters with inelegant, square-shaped structures.

The famous German ace Manfred von Richthofen, better known as the Red Baron, flew an Albatros before he discovered the Fokker Dr.1, the plane with which he is most associated. However, he was critical of the final version of the Albatros, the D-V, and instead preferred the earlier D-III, though it exhibited some lower-wing weakness during steep turns or dives. Albatros fighters enjoyed an intensive but short production run, with thousands produced in two years.

The Albatros looked like no other World War I fighter—its unique semimonocoque fuselage made of formed plywood gave it a svelte aerodynamic shape. But structural problems with its wings led to healthy skepticism among Albatros pilots.

AVIAT HUSKY

Carved and perfected in the deep rustic country of western Wyoming, the Aviat Husky first emerged from that setting in the late 1980s as a backcountry pilot's dream machine. Frank Christensen, designer of the Eagle aerobatic biplane, liked the look and the performance of the Piper Super Cub, which was out of production. Inspired by the Super Cub, he came up with his own design: the Husky, which retained all the fun-flying characteristics of the popular Piper taildragger while providing a slew of new capabilities. For instance, it has 60-percent-span flaps, meaning the high-lift surfaces extend almost two-thirds of the way from wing root to wingtip for greatly improved short takeoff and landing performance.

The current Husky models are available with flat-panel instrumentation and navigation equipment that can make old-school bush pilots turn green with envy. Compared with its forebears, a Husky goes farther, climbs faster, and packs more payload. And with oversize tundra tires, it's perfectly at home on the shortest and roughest of backcountry airstrips. Whether the destination is a grassy meadow amid the mountains, a glacier in Alaska, or a rocky sandbar along a narrow river bed, the Husky will not only get there, it'll ensure a fun ride along the way. Though Frank Christensen eventually sold the company, it is still based in Afton, Wyoming. It now operates under the name Aviat Aircraft.

Because of its great visibility, handling ability, and slow-flight capabilities, the Husky is a popular utility airplane. It's even used by the Kenya Wildlife Service to patrol against poachers.

MCDONNELL DOUGLAS F-15 EAGLE

When it first arrived on the scene at the height of the Cold War, the F-15 constituted a quantum leap in fighter technology. The single-seat tactical fighter could outmaneuver any aircraft flying at the time, whether friend or foe. Its development was spurred by the mistaken fear that the Soviet MiG-25—the airplane the F-15 would likely meet in combat—was a maneuverable dogfighter. In fact, the Russian aircraft was designed to be a high-speed interceptor, but McDonnell Douglas's efforts to develop a highly maneuverable aircraft weren't without payoff: They ended up creating one of the most effective fighter jets in history.

The F-15's advanced avionics gave pilots the new ability to operate radar and missile systems without ever taking their hands off the airplane's controls. The primary control levers were studded with dozens of knobs and switches, and pilots learned to manipulate them intuitively, like a musician playing an instrument.

Stan Whitfield, former F-15 pilot and 58th Fighter Squadron Operations Officer during Operation Desert Storm, said that flying the F-15 was an unparalleled experience: "I felt like I was on top of the world flying the F-15 Eagle. The combination of precise fingertip control and the raw power of full afterburner—which felt like a kick in the pants—left me with a big smile on my face after every flight." That afterburner power allowed the airplane to pitch up more than 60 degrees as it climbed to 20,000 feet (6,096 m) in a short distance. With more than one hundred victories and no losses, no fighter past or present has been able to match the F-15 Eagle's record of air-to-air combat effectiveness.

Some skeptics were concerned that the F-15 Eagle's large size would make it difficult to maneuver effectively in a dogfight—in fact, its massiveness earned it the nickname the Tennis Court. But it's never been bested.

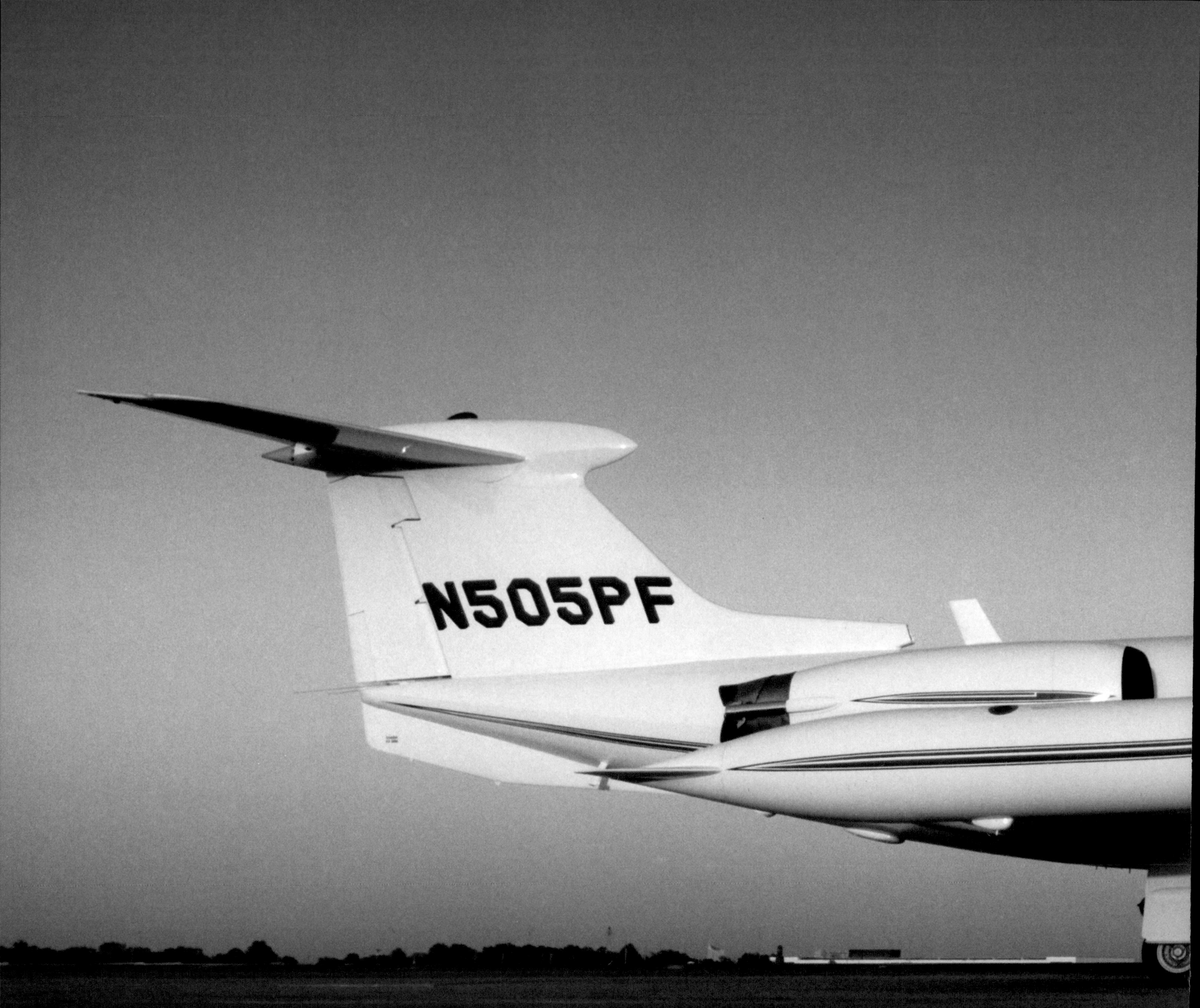
N505PF

One could joke that the eccentric visionary William Powell ("Bill") Lear extracted the DNA from an obscure Swiss jet-fighter design and moved the works to Wichita, Kansas. That's where the pure turbojet Lear 23 was born, and it changed the face of aviation: Within a few years of its first delivery in 1964, the Learjet became synonymous with *business jet*. The aircraft was sexy and fast with a speed of 518 miles per hour (833.75 km/h). Plus it could climb more than 6,000 feet (1,828.75 m) per minute and cover a range of around 1,727 miles (2,779.5 km). Though just 104 Lear 23s were built before production ceased in 1966, the airplane formed the basis for a long lineup of Lears, a family that lives on.

The Lear was said to be a handful to fly and was allegedly vulnerable to "Mach tuck," a condition in which the jet became less stable the higher and faster it flew. The airflow over the top of the wing could exceed the speed of sound, leading to a shock wave and causing a loss of control. Bill Lear responded to this flaw with the Learjet 24, which had better handling abilities at high speed.

Today, Learjet is owned by Canadian company Bombardier. But back in the early days, Bill Lear's larger-than-life character was part of the 23's identity. His energy and excesses are as much a part of the Learjet story as its accomplishments in engineering. He also never missed a chance to defend against critics. When someone complained, "You can't stand up in a Learjet cabin," Lear countered that you can't stand up in the back of a limo, either. The developmental U.S.$17.2 million, all-composite Learjet 85 is the latest version to emerge from Lear's original design.

The trim lines and sharp nose of the original Learjet—the Model 23, introduced in 1964—remain the identifying points of succeeding models to this very day.

ENGINE INNOVATIONS

Without engines, flight would never have gone far. The first powered aircraft, the *Wright Flyer* of 1903, was achieved with a 12-horsepower engine just barely strong enough to get it airborne. Today, solid-fuel rocket engines can produce more than 2 million pounds (907 mt) of thrust, allowing us to send huge payloads into space, but there has been propulsion progress in all facets of aviation, and there continue to be improvements every day. Here are some of the highlights of the march of power-plant progress.

PROPELLER DISC
ON CRANKSHAFT

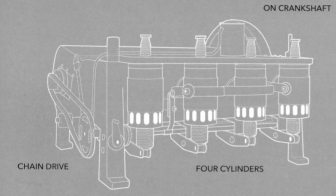

CHAIN DRIVE

FOUR CYLINDERS

1915

Curtiss OX-5 V-8 – Glenn H. Curtiss

The Curtiss OX-5 V-8 aircraft engine has gone down in aviation lore as a legendary power plant. Curtiss introduced the OX-5 in 1910, and it soon found its way into the JN-4 Jenny, another Curtiss product. Over the next decade, he built more than 12,000 of these pretty V-8s, which were capable of producing a mere 90 horsepower and which also had a well-earned reputation for giving up the ghost at the worst possible moment. It would, however, set the stage for the great V-8 and V-12 piston engines of the World War II era.

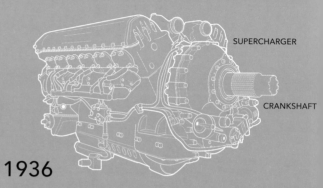

SUPERCHARGER

CRANKSHAFT

1936

Rolls-Royce Merlin – Rolls-Royce

The Merlin produces that most magical sound of airplanes in flight: the humming roar of twelve cylinders in perfect harmony at an easy, deep-throated gallop. It's powered dozens of airplanes, including the Supermarine Spitfire, and a licensed version made by Packard helped create the ultimate WWII fighter, the North American P-51D Mustang. Its two-speed superchargers gave the Mustang the range necessary to watch over B-17 bombers as they made their way deep into German-held territory.

1903

Wright Flyer Engine – Charles Taylor

Arguably the most noteworthy engine in aviation history was a low-powered handmade model built by the Wright brothers' ace mechanic Charlie Taylor. Packaged in an innovative all-aluminum crankcase with a chain drive to spin the propellers, that primitive four-banger provided the 12 horsepower needed to just barely get the *Wright Flyer* airborne on December 17, 1903.

1931

Continental A-40 – Continental Motors

In the early 1930s, when the Great Depression made it difficult to develop low-cost yet reliable engines for light aircraft, Continental Motors came up with the first engine in a lineup of products that would eventually power tens of thousands of light airplanes around the world. The A-40—a two-cylinder, 40-horsepower opposed engine (meaning its cylinders come from either side of the case)—is arguably the best known of these, as it powered the first Piper Cub and led to the development of a line of engines that powered many thousands of aircraft over the next eighty-plus years.

1910

Le Rhone Rotary – Louis, Laurent, and Augustin Seguin

Believe it or not, the most common engines in World War I airplanes had their entire bank of cylinders rotating around the crankshaft. These Le Rhone "rotary" engines, as they are known, were first developed for airplanes by the Seguin brothers of Gnome et Rhône, and they provided good amounts of horsepower at relatively light weights and with good cooling. They were an all-or-nothing affair, however—full power or none at all with the pilot intermittently turning the ignition off and back on again—and they routinely sprayed pilots with mineral oil as part of the experience. By the 1920s, the rotary was dead.

CYLINDER

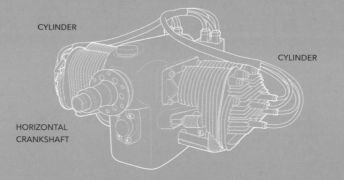

CYLINDER

HORIZONTAL
CRANKSHAFT

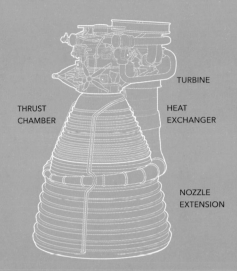

TURBINE

THRUST
CHAMBER

HEAT
EXCHANGER

NOZZLE
EXTENSION

1953

Lycoming O-320 – Lycoming

The little four-cylinder engine from Pennsylvania manufacturer Lycoming epitomizes the light airplane engine, helped by the fact that it powered the most popular light planes ever, such as the Cessna 172 and Piper PA-28 Cherokee. With four cylinders arrayed two on each side, big air-cooled heads helping cool the cylinders, a normally carbureted fuel system, and a dual magneto ignition all driving a fixed-blade prop, the O-320 was 1930s design updated with the latest materials and manufacturing techniques. The bottom line: The O-320 delivers reliability, affordability, and familiarity.

1960s

Rocketdyne F-1 Liquid-Fueled Rocket Engine – Rocketdyne

Despite its relative antiquity, the F-1, which dates to the late 1950s, remains the most powerful liquid-fueled propulsion system ever built, putting out 1.5 million pounds (680.5 mt) of thrust. Five F-1s were used for each Saturn V launch, the rocket program that landed us on the moon. Each engine burned more than 400 gallons (1,514.25 L) of liquid oxygen per second, approximately 5,000 times the amount of a high-powered jet engine used on commercial airliners today.

1988

Williams FJ44 – Williams International

Introduced by Williams International, a then-little-known manufacturer of cruise missile engines, the Williams FJ44 would become the epitome of modern very-light-jet engine design. Popularized on the prolific Cessna CitationJet lineup, the FJ44 proved itself a reliable and efficient performer, to the point that improved versions boast nearly double the thrust rating of the original and have remained stellar performers in the category a quarter of a century after the engine's introduction.

1963

Pratt & Whitney Canada PT6 – Pratt & Whitney Canada

Over the past six decades, the Pratt & Whitney Canada PT6 engine has become the gold standard in the turboprop world. Its two independent turbines are easily separated, making for easy installation and maintenance, and its efficient propulsion turns fuel into thrust in the thinner, breathable altitudes at 30,000 feet (9,144 m). P&WC says that, out of the 46,000 engines it's delivered since the '60s, more than 26,000 are still flying today, attesting to the engine's reliability, quality design and manufacturing, and ease of repair.

1974

CFM International CFM56 – General Electric & Snecma

In a joint venture between General Electric and French company Snecma, the CFM56 was launched in the mid-1970s and has become one of the most-produced jet engines—thanks to its adoption by Boeing in the 737, which became the best-selling airliner. The CFM56 is a high-bypass ratio turbofan, which means that most of the air that goes into the engine bypasses the turbine section and instead powers the engine's huge spinning fan. High-bypass design means higher fuel efficiency, lighter weight, and much quieter performance—all hallmarks of modern jet aviation.

FAN SECTION

TURBINE

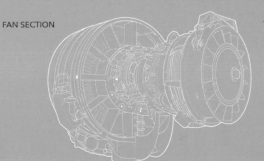

JUNKERS JU-52

In 1932, Adolf Hitler awed the German public by chartering a Lufthansa Junkers Ju-52 while campaigning for chancellor. The image of a candidate traveling by air, rather than by train, helped deceive Depression-ridden Germany into believing that Hitler was a modern man with the vision to pull them out of the depths of national despair.

The big trimotor transport represented the best of German technology at the time. It was all metal, a construction technique pioneered by German designers during World War I. It had a full-cantilever wing, meaning it was entirely supported by its internal structure and needed no external struts or wires. In an age when many aircraft still flew with open cockpits, the Ju-52 had a large, comfortable, enclosed cabin. Like its high-wing cousin across the Atlantic, the Ford Tri-Motor, the Ju-52 used corrugated aluminum skin for

added strength. Initially the Ju-52 was conceived as a single-engine ship, but it proved to be underpowered with just one engine: Two wing-mounted engines were added and the classic configuration was established. The Ju-52 first flew with a 770-horsepower Pratt & Whitney Hornet radial engine, which— ironically—was developed by the Americans. Later it employed BMW 132s, a refined copy of the Hornet built in Germany under license.

Ju-52s figured prominently in the secret growth of Hitler's Luftwaffe. Though presented publicly as an airliner, they were stealthily fitted with bomb-bay doors and defensive machine guns. Ju-52s served during World War II as bombers, transports, and paratrooper delivery vehicles, as well as personal transport for the führer. As of 2008, eight airworthy Ju-52s were still operating, with another fifteen or so in storage or on display.

Though the Ju-52 was rugged, reliable, and easy to fly, it was also a bit slow, making it somewhat vulnerable to attack during combat.

NORTH AMERICAN AT-6 TEXAN

Fighter pilots may be born to serve, but they still need training. North American's AT-6 Texan was nicknamed the Pilotmaker because it filled just that purpose. During World War II, army pilot training came in three phases: primary, basic, and advanced. After basic, most cadets became bomber or transport pilots and went on to advanced training in twin-engine aircraft. Others were deemed the elite—the fighter jocks—and they learned to man the AT-6.

North American Aviation began producing the AT-6 in the late 1930s, right in time for it to assume its training role before the start of World War II. The U.S. Army Air Forces dubbed it the Texan. To naval aviators, it was the SNJ, and pilots training in the United Kingdom and its territories called the AT-6 the Harvard.

Its range of nicknames isn't surprising considering how widely the airplanes are flown: The more than 15,000 built have been used in more than fifty nations, including Haiti, Nicaragua, Turkey, and the former Yugoslavia. Norm Goyer, an AT-6 owner and restorer, said, "If you could fly an AT-6, you could fly any fighter in the world. The Texan had a perfect match of power, weight, and control effectiveness." One of North American's most enduring success stories, the AT-6 remains popular among warbird owners and air-show performers today.

Today, many Texans are maintained and operated by nostalgic enthusiasts. The plane's loud radial engine and noisy propeller make it a favorite at air shows.

SPIRIT OF ST. LOUIS

Charles Lindbergh was an ex–airmail pilot who first mused about making a transatlantic flight during the boring hours he spent flying his routes. Eventually, that dream came true: He flew the *Spirit of St. Louis* (a highly modified Ryan M-2 single-engine mail airplane) solo across the Atlantic in May 1927. But Lindbergh didn't just fly the model—he also helped Ryan Aircraft's Donald Hall design the plane that made the young pilot one of the world's first media sensations. His record-breaking flight showed that airplanes were more than a barnstorming sideshow and had potential for viable transatlantic transportation.

The *Spirit*'s fuselage was essentially an array of five flying fuel tanks holding a total of 450 gallons (1,703.5 L). The two largest tanks were located in front of the cockpit, so Lindbergh had to either slip the airplane— allowing it to momentarily move somewhat sideways as well as forward— or use a periscope to see ahead. In addition, the Wright Whirlwind J-5C engine, which was built in Paterson, New Jersey, was as much of a technological marvel as the airplane it powered. With 223 horsepower, its reliability gave Lindbergh and his backers confidence that the *Spirit of St. Louis* could endure the 3,610 miles (5,809.75 km) he flew in thirty-three hours and thirty minutes from New York to Paris.

Several replicas of the airplane have flown, but the original hangs in the Smithsonian National Air and Space Museum in Washington, D.C. In his later years, Lindbergh is said to have visited the museum often, sitting in the cockpit when the plane was lowered for cleaning and recalling the flight that defined his career and set the tone for all of aviation for decades to come.

The *Spirit of St. Louis* didn't just change the course of aviation history. It also won Lindbergh the U.S.$25,000 Orteig Prize for the first nonstop flight between New York and Paris.

PIPER PA-32 CHEROKEE SIX

A stretched version of the Piper Cherokee was an idea that came early to the folks in Vero Beach, Florida, and the result, the PA-32 Cherokee Six, was a huge hit. Piper built nearly 8,000 PA-32s. The first ones came with a 260-horsepower engine, which most owners agreed was just not enough for the large size of the cabin. Thus, power was increased to 300 horsepower. Piper's next move was to add a retractable-gear model, and the version of the airplane called the Lance was born.

In all, there have been more than a dozen variants of the original Piper Cherokee manufactured, including a factory-built floatplane version. Among the major improvements along the way was a tapered wing, which added complexity to the production process but greatly improved aerodynamic efficiency. There are also turbocharged versions for owners with high-altitude missions.

With seating for six, the PA-32 is a marvelous family airplane that outdoes its rivals in size, space, and comfort. It also has a wide cabin door for pilots as well as a generous side door for boarding passengers—travelers feel like they're climbing aboard a substantial cruiser, which means a lot for the success of small charter operators. Not fast, at around 160 miles per hour (257.5 km/h) for the fixed-gear, 300-horsepower model, the Six makes up for it with a prodigious useful load and easy Cherokee flyability.

The early models of the Piper Cherokee Six feature Piper's classic rectangular platform wing, popularly called the "Hershey bar" wing because of its resemblance to the rectangular chocolate bar.

QUICKSILVER MX-2

Just as the famous compact and low-powered Cubs, Taylorcrafts, and Aeroncas did in the 1930s, the planes of the 1980s ultralight craze promised to bring flight to the masses. Though derided as "flying lawn chairs," ultralights had the potential to be perfectly airworthy magic carpets as long as they were flown within their limitations: warm weather without much wind. They were epitomized by easy-to-fly and simple-to-build-at-home designs so affordable that almost anyone could own one. Exemplifying that principle were the Eipper Quicksilver models, especially the MX line. Eipper was founded by Dick Eipper, who whimsically named his company "Eipper Formance."

Designed by Bob Lovejoy, the Quicksilver models were the most popular airplanes in the world for a time. At the height of the ultralight movement, the company was shipping hundreds of airplane kits per month to eager home-builders. With high-lift wings (sacrificing top-end speed), it didn't take much thrust to make the MX-2 fly—and cheap, low-horsepower engines were widely available, spurring the fad. To date, the various Quicksilver manufacturers have turned out more than 14,000 sport airplanes, the vast majority of them characterized by simple aluminum tube-and-sailcloth construction, two-stroke engines, and very low speeds, along with the highest fun-to-weight ratio in the sky.

While employing simple construction and materials, ultralights offer a fun flying experience. The MX-2 offered side-by-side seating for two.

MITSUBISHI A6M ZERO

The Mitsubishi Zero epitomized Japan's World War II air capabilities more than any other aircraft. Renowned for its strength as a dogfighter, the lightweight, agile airplane was the first naval fighter that could outperform land aircraft. Its great range is what made the attack on Pearl Harbor feasible: The bombers and torpedo planes of the Japanese Imperial Navy employed it as a fighter escort. The Zero would see prolific use throughout the war, as a total of approximately 11,000 of the fighters were produced through 1945—the most by far of any Japanese airplane.

Capable of reaching speeds up to 350 miles per hour (563.25 km/h) and with a range just shy of 2,000 miles (3,218.75 km), the aircraft gave the Japanese an early upper hand in combat over the American Army's Curtiss P-40s and the Navy's Grumman F4F Wildcats.

General Claire Chennault, commander of the American Volunteer Group in China, the Flying Tigers, advised his pilots against trying to outmaneuver the Zero in their heavier, less agile P-40s. Instead, he told pilots to avoid combat unless they had the altitude advantage. When they did, their orders were to dive on the Zero, exploit its lack of armor plate and self-sealing fuel tanks, and use the P-40's speed to zoom back up for another pass. Later American fighters like the Chance-Vought Corsair and the Grumman F6F Hellcat spelled a certain end to the Zero's edge.

The sleek lines and unique construction of the Mitsubishi Zero fighter gave the Japanese the upper hand in the early days of World War II's Pacific Theater. The feared Zero got its name from the last digit of the Japanese Imperial Year 2600 (1940), which was when it was introduced.

AERO COMMANDER

The design of the Aero Commander, later called the Shrike Commander and Twin Commander, was way ahead of its time when former Douglas Aircraft engineer Ted Smith conceived of the craft in the late 1940s. What was initially planned as a light twin-engine airplane with 260-horsepower engines evolved through increasingly larger, more powerful versions, ultimately morphing into the Jet Commander.

Smith's signature design format was the high- or mid-wing configuration, with the long main landing gear legs attached under the wings at the engine mounts. The Aero Commander had a low-slung look on the ground, with its belly resting just above the pavement. While designed as a twin, the airplane's performance with only one engine running was one of its selling points, so much so that Aero Design and Engineering Company (the company formed to build the Commander) organized a demonstration flight from Oklahoma City, Oklahoma, to Washington, D.C., using only one of its engines. Its stellar performance earned it a spot serving as Air Force One for President Dwight Eisenhower. And while it was being marketed by North American Aviation, the Shrike Commander achieved lasting fame at the hands of demonstration pilot and aerobatic phenom Bob Hoover. Later models featured turboprops boasting as much as 820 horsepower and, finally, jet engines mounted on pylons near the tail.

The Aero Commander is a rugged and capable twin-engine multirole aircraft that was continuously upgraded over the years.

KITFOX

In the early 1980s, simplified-construction airplane kits for building at home became all the rage, and Dan Denney's Kitfox—a little model with two side-by-side seats—was the hottest home-built airplane going. The design was a basic high-wing strutted monoplane with a fuselage skeleton of welded steel tubing. The wings had wood spars and aluminum ribs, and the whole airplane was covered in fabric. It was a design format right out of the 1930s, but with a number of modern innovations that made the Kitfox lighter and more reliable than its ancestors.

One of those touches—folding wings—made the Kitfox attractive as a kit, compact and simple enough to assemble in a two-car garage and then transport with a trailer to and from the airport. Another selling point was the round, bumped cowling shipped with most Kitfox kits. It gave the airplane a classic look, recalling light airplanes of the 1930s Golden Age, specifically the Monocoupe—even though the developmental radial engine that Denney had designed the cowling to fit over never made it off the drawing board. In addition to its round cowl, the Kitfox also had flaperons: detachable trailing-edge devices that serve as both ailerons and flaps.

At one point, Denney Aerocraft was turning out more than fifty Kitfox kits a month. Though nearly 5,000 kits have been delivered, it's hard to know how many have actually flown.

With looks harking back to aviation's Golden Age in the 1930s—plus retro touches like the raised, painted bumps on its cowl—the Kitfox was a huge and immediate success when it arrived in 1984.

DASSAULT FALCON 7X

The Dassault Falcon 7X holds many notable distinctions—two of the most important are its status as the first fully fly-by-wire business jet (meaning its manual controls are replaced by an electronic interface) and the fact that it is the first plane to be designed entirely on a virtual platform with Catia's engineering software. In some ways, the twenty-first–century design and tooling process that created the Falcon rivals the advanced technology of the airplane it produced: Engineers throughout the world were able to share images and information in real time with Dassault Falcon team leaders in Paris and on the assembly lines in Bordeaux as work progressed. Three-dimensional screen images were created of all parts and assemblies, including the use

of computerized virtual workmen crawling through tight spots or turning wrenches in tight quarters, the better to envision maintenance and repair operations and change the location of parts if they proved not easily accessible.

The resulting airplane is Dassault's flagship model, combining its tri-jet configuration (a hallmark of the French airframer) with a high cruise speed, a range of nearly 6,000 nautical miles (11,112 km), and a roomy cabin. Avionics consist of Dassault's award-winning EASy cockpit, derived from the Honeywell Primus Epic platform and optimized for the 7X. Unveiled in 2005 at the Paris Air Show, the model gained FAA and EASA-type certification in 2007. Among the first customers was company president Serge Dassault.

The Falcon 7X was the first Dassault-built business jet to incorporate winglets for improved aerodynamic efficiency and mobility.

VOUGHT F4U CORSAIR

The single-seat F4U Corsair was intended from its conception for carrier duty, ingeniously designed with its inverted gull-wing shape for extra propeller clearance and sturdy landing-gear support. Yet the original Corsair, with its long nose, stiff landing gear, and large three-blade propeller, proved difficult for pilots to land on carrier decks—to the point that attempting to do so was downright dangerous.

As a result, Corsairs deployed in the early days of World War II were assigned to shore-based squadrons in the Pacific. Many went to marine corps squadrons, which had always been cursed with the regular Navy's castoff equipment. Now they received a cutting-edge fighter with the latest, most powerful engine and a rugged construction that would serve the marines well. In later Corsair models, a shorter-diameter, four-blade propeller, redesigned cockpit seat, new canopy, and updated landing gear solved the Corsair's initial shortcomings.

The redesigned airplane went on to prove its fighting acumen in battle, proving itself the most formidable carrier-based bomber of the war and achieving an 11:1 victory ratio over the Japanese Zero fighters it battled. It's been reported that some Japanese pilots thought of the Corsair as the most threatening American fighter in the air. In addition to the U.S. military, the aircraft has been employed by the Royal New Zealand Air Force and the French Navy.

The model for countless schoolboy doodles, Vought's bent-wing F4U Corsair was one of the most successful fighters in the Pacific Theater of World War II.

NORTHROP GRUMMAN B-2 STEALTH BOMBER

Development of the Northrop B-2 bomber began in the 1970s when the Pentagon sought a replacement for the Boeing B-52 Stratofortress. Northrop Grumman and Boeing spent more than a decade and billions of dollars developing the stealth bomber with a flying wing that uses angular faceting and other technologies to reduce its radar signature.

It is poetic justice that Northrop was involved with the B-2: Just after World War II, before radar transparency was considered an issue, ahead-of-the-curve company founder Jack Northrop envisioned flying-wing technology as the wave of the future. Starting with small single-pilot aircraft, he built up to the giant YB-49, a jet-powered competitor to Convair's piston/jet hybrid B-36. However, conservatism won out, and the radical Northrop design never went into production.

The concept was reborn decades later in the stealth B-2. The B-2's radar-absorbent coating is so sensitive that the bombers must be kept in spotlessly clean hangars with precision-controlled temperature and humidity. The winding down of the Cold War led Congress to slash B-2 orders from 132 to twenty-one. A total of twenty remain in service with the U.S. Air Force after the 2008 crash of a B-2 on the runway in Guam, where the crew safely ejected.

The Northrop Grumman B-2 Bomber can slice through hostile airspace without being detected by radar. It's a flying-wing aircraft, meaning it has no fuselage or tail, making it highly aerodynamic to boot.

GOSSAMER ALBATROSS

Designed by aeronautical engineer Paul MacCready, the *Gossamer Albatross* was a leg-powered airplane that, in 1979, made the first human-powered flight across the English Channel. That 22¼-mile (35.75-km) flight covered roughly the same distance flown by Louis Blériot—the first pilot to cross the Channel in an airplane—seven decades earlier.

Piloted by cyclist Bryan Allen, the *Albatross* made the trip in two hours and forty-nine minutes, at an average speed of 18 miles per hour (29 km/h) and soaring approximately 5 feet (1.5 m) above the waves. The accomplishment won MacCready's team the Kremer prize of £100,000 (U.S.$210,000).

Two years earlier, the team had won its first Kremer Prize of £50,000 (U.S.$86,000) for the first human-powered aircraft, the *Gossamer Condor*. The further-evolved *Albatross*, constructed of carbon fiber with a strong yet light Mylar covering and a wingspan of nearly 100 feet (30.5 m), weighed just 71 pounds (32.25 kg) empty. Its all-up weight was approximately 220 pounds (99.75 kg) when it took off on its flight across the Channel. The long tapered wings, like those of a glider, were designed to require a minimum amount of power to keep the *Albatross* aloft. In still air, the pilot needed to produce the equivalent of approximately 0.4 horsepower by pedaling to drive the two-blade pusher propeller. Any amount of turbulence, however, required much more energy. MacCready's team brought the work of forward-thinking aircraft designers to the attention of the world and opened people's eyes to the exciting, wide-open future of flight.

The *Albatross* was flown inside the Houston Astrodome, making it the first controlled indoor flight by a human-powered aircraft. Only two of the models were built.

EXTRA 300

The brainchild of modern composite guru Walter Extra of Germany, the Extra 300 burst onto the scene in the early 1990s as the ultimate competitive aerobat. In a field dominated by stubby, high-powered biplanes, the sleek Extra 300 monoplane was a game changer. Available in either a factory built certificated version or as a build-it-yourself kit-plane, the 300 is incredibly quick, nimble, and strong. It's certified to plus/minus 10 Gs—legally able to withstand the force of ten times its weight whether right side up or upside down—but is actually thought to be much stronger. Its strength, agility, and sleek aerodynamics allowed competitors to perform rolls and dives like no one had ever attempted.

The 300's fuselage is made of a skeleton of welded steel tubing, but the wing is made from a carbon-fiber main spar covered in composite skin. The wing is symmetrical, meaning it has no curve on the upper surface. That design permits the Extra 300 to fly as well inverted as it does right side up.

Walter Extra's wonderplane established itself as a huge force in the world of aerobatic competition, pushing the state of the art to new heights. Flown by aerobatics legends Patty Wagstaff and Michael Goulian in air shows and competitions throughout the world, and eventually popularized through its representation in Microsoft's Flight Simulator, the 300 became the embodiment of the aerobatic monoplane.

With a wing that has withstood 20 Gs of stress in testing, the Extra 300 can handle anything modern aerobatic pilots can throw at it—including flying incredibly well when upside down, as shown above.

CESSNA CITATIONJET

When Cessna introduced the model 525 CitationJet in the early 1990s, it was an attempt by the company to get back to its roots as makers of the ultimate entry-level bizjet. Its new jet, known affectionately as the CJ, was a well-sized, single-pilot-friendly jet. Though the fuselage measured 11 inches (28 cm) shorter than that of the Citation I it was replacing, the CJ had a lowered center aisle and thus had more headroom than its ancestor.

The entire CJ line was made possible in part by a new class of small turbofan engines from Williams International. Dr. Sam Williams initially designed the turbofans to power long-range cruise missiles, but then he turned his attention to light passenger jets. The CitationJet was the first large-scale-production passenger jet to use Williams's new type of engine, and it would go on not only to great sales success, with hundreds sold, but also to spawn an entire line of light jets up to the 2,000-mile- (3,218.75-km-) range Citation CJ4.

At the lower end, Cessna subsequently developed the Citation Mustang light jet to reestablish its commitment to owner-pilots. Today, the spirit of the CJ lives on in the form of Cessna's new M2, with flat-panel displays, a speed of 400 miles per hour (643.75 km/h), and high-end interiors.

The Cessna CitationJet's distinctive T-tail was a brand-new feature, a departure from the tail design of the Cessna Citation I. This new arrangement raised the tail so that it no longer obstructed the airflow from the wings, resulting in a smoother ride in its high-ceilinged cabin.

MIKOYAN-GUREVICH MIG-15

The first time American fighter pilots in Korea encountered a certain new Soviet jet fighter, they were shocked by its speed. That fighter, the MiG-15, was developed by the design team of Artem Mikoyan and mathematician Mikhail Gurevich—thus the designation MiG (the lower-case *i* representing the Russian word for *and*). It was the first Soviet jet fighter with drag-reducing swept wings, and it took the measure of the Allies' straight-wing jets in combat. It wasn't until the arrival of the swept-wing North American F-86 Sabre that American pilots could compete on equal terms.

The Klimov RD-45 engine powering the MiG-15 was a reverse-engineered copy of the British Rolls-Royce Nene jet engine. Remarkably, the British government had offered the Russians the rights to build the Rolls-inspired engine under license, though with the ensuing Cold War, no royalties were ever paid. In addition, the Soviets learned from seized German research documents that swept wings would enhance performance while flying at transonic speeds, or speeds near the speed of sound. The MiG-15 benefited from that knowledge, and its performance was a big surprise for unsuspecting opponents in the early days of the Korean War.

The North Korean Air Force introduced the MiG-15 to combat, though it is widely believed that many MiGs were actually flown in combat by Russian pilots. American pilots would return from dogfights claiming they had gotten so close to their adversaries in the air that they could see that their eyes were blue—and that they could hear Russian curse words over the radio.

РОМАН ВАРШАВСКИЙ

To avoid high-altitude condensation trails that would give away their positions, MiG-15 pilots on their way into Korea would climb high enough to begin generating a contrail, then drop down just below condensation levels to become less visible.

CESSNA 210/P210

The Cessna 210 series became popular for its ability to carry a hefty payload; take off and land on short, rugged strips; fly a long way; and exhibit stability and reliability while doing so. The series evolved from 1957 through 1985, and the airplanes built at the end of the run are barely recognizable as being from the same series as the first ones. The original 210s incorporated retractable landing gear, a swept tail, and a new wing design. They had four seats and a tame 260-horsepower Continental engine, and the wing still featured the familiar Cessna struts.

The endcap on the evolution of the series was the 1985 Cessna P210, which was a six-seat, pressurized, serious flying machine with a 325-horsepower engine, de-ice boots, and high-altitude capability. Only forty of these P210 models were built, and they're prized on today's used aircraft market for their capabilities as well as for their rarity. Between '57 and '85, twenty-four different versions featured progressive improvements. For instance, the T210s were turbocharged and P210s were pressurized.

On the used airplane market, 210s have traditionally been considered to have among the best performance, range, and load-carrying capability for the money. Today they're high-performance airplanes without the high-performance price tags, and they remain popular in the roles of family airplane, air taxi, and corporate transportation craft for small companies.

In 1982, Canadian pilots Don Muir and André Daemon set a world record for traveling around the world in a single-engine plane. They accomplished it in six days in their trusty Cessna 210.

The oval fuselage and steep 36-degree swept wing of Gulfstream's G650 help make it one of the most luxurious and graceful of the high-performance business jets in the air.

GULFSTREAM G650

Gulfstream is probably the most recognizable private jet brand in the field of ultimate personal transport. Beginning with the Gulfstream II, the manufacturer's first jet-powered model, the line has consistently offered long-range, wide-body comfort and performance. Whether its planes are used as business tools or as transportation for celebrities, the name Gulfstream has long signified the top of the line.

An outstanding performer all around, the newest Gulfstream G650 combines a top speed close to the speed of sound with a range of 8,050 miles (12,955.25 km). It has the widest, tallest, and longest cabin in its class, and is the first Gulfstream to expand on the cabin cross-section that was originally designed in 1966. The G650 achieves its remarkable performance thanks to a sleek, aerodynamically optimized fuselage and its new Rolls-Royce BR725 turbofan engines, which provide more thrust and better fuel efficiency than previous-generation engines. Pilots operate the aircraft via a fly-by-wire, entirely electronic control system, which is common in commercial airliners but still relatively rare in private aircraft. If you want one, you'd better start saving now—the list price is a cool U.S.$64.5 million.

CESSNA 182 SKYLANE

Cessna introduced the Model 182 Skylane in 1956, shortly after the birth of its all-time sales champ, the 172 Skyhawk. Very similar in appearance, both planes have strutted high wings, fixed tricycle landing gear, and a tall, easy-to-access cabin. But the Skylane is arguably a better airplane: With a bigger cabin, more power, and a constant-speed propeller, it hauls more, goes faster, has better range, and still needs precious little runway. Both are marvelously simple to fly and so stable that autopilot sometimes seems like a waste of panel space.

The 182's 235-horsepower engine burns slightly more fuel than the 172's engine does, but it seems well worth it. There have been many variants of the Skylane over the years, including retractable-gear versions. When Cessna resumed production of light aircraft in 1996 after more than a decade of idle assembly lines, the Skylane was among the first models reintroduced.

Despite its 1956 heritage, today's version is a very modern airplane: Its panel is dominated by Garmin flat-screen avionics, including traffic alerting, onboard satellite weather, and synthetic vision. The engine is fuel-injected, the seat belts incorporate airbags, and the energy-absorbing seats are designed to protect occupants in a crash landing. Its impressive payload, range, comfort, and visibility have helped make the Skylane one of the best-selling singles of all time.

The Cessna 182 Skylane is made mostly of aluminum alloy, though some parts—like the wheel covers and wingtips—are made of thermoplastic material or Fiberglas.

ANTONOV AN-225 MRIYA

Size matters, and the Antonov An-225 *Mriya* (the Ukranian word for "dream") is simply the largest operational aircraft in the world. Its 290-foot (88.5-m) wingspan is second only to the Hughes H-4 Hercules, better known as the *Spruce Goose*. But the *Mriya* is longer than the H-4 and it remains in regular service, while the *Spruce Goose* flew only once just above Long Beach Harbor.

The An-225 was developed as an expanded version of the four-engine An-124, specifically to piggyback the Buran, the Soviet version of the space shuttle. It carried the Buran spacecraft to the Paris Air Show in 1989 and holds the world record for airlifted payload—418,834 pounds (190 mt).

Even after the collapse of the Soviet Union in 1991 and the cessation of the Buran space program, the An-225 continues to operate as an international cargo superstar. Only one exists (although a second is reportedly under construction), and it flew for the first time in 1988. Distinguishing design features include seven double-wheel landing-gear legs mounted on each side of the fuselage for a total of twenty-eight main landing gear tires. The cargo hold is cavernous enough to have contained the entire first flight of the *Wright Flyer*. In addition, the Canadian and U.S. governments have both chartered the *Mriya* to carry supplies to coalition forces in the Middle East.

The Antonov An-225's cavernous cargo compartment (shown here with its door open) has lifted the heaviest item ever sent through the air: a generator for a gas power plant in Armenia.

ANTONOV
DESIGN BUREAU
INTERNATIONAL CARGO
TRANSPORTER
Phone:38(044)454-28-60
Fax:38(044)454-28-52
E-mail:office@antonov.kiev.ua

GRANVILLE BROTHERS GEE BEE R SERIES

The same people who look at a yellow-and-black bumblebee and say, "How does it fly?" probably have a similar reaction to the Gee Bee Model R-1 and R-2 racers. Made for the 1932 racing season by Granville Brothers Aircraft of Springfield, Massachusetts, the Model R sister ships were built on the success of the previous year's Thompson Trophy–winning Model Z. Dubbed Gee Bees (for "Granville Brothers," referring to partners Zantford, Thomas, Robert, Mark, and Edward Granville), the racers had the look of a flying beer barrel with stubby wings. The R-1 was powered by an enormous Pratt & Whitney R-1340 radial engine, while the R-2 sported a slightly smaller R-985. The pilot's seat was far back, practically inside the tail, for balance—and so that he could see race course pylons during a steep turn. The plane's huge, aerodynamic wheel spats further contributed to its ungainly appearance.

But the Gee Bee's designers had performed wind-tunnel tests, and their theory of aerodynamic shape produced winning speed numbers. In addition, the teardrop shape of the body provided enough lift of its own that the Gee Bee could be flown on its side (called "knife-edge" flight). Jimmy Doolittle, later famous for his B-25 raid on Japan in the early days of World War II, won the 1932 Thompson Trophy race in a Gee Bee R-1 and set a speed record of 296 miles per hour (476.5 km/h). He praised the Gee Bee as "the sweetest ship I've ever flown." But Gee Bees were infamous for their spectacular and fatal crashes, leading to their reputation as airplanes for only the most expert of pilots. Russell Boardman crashed to his death during the 1933 cross-country Bendix Trophy race, and before that, in 1931, Lowell Bayles was killed in a Model Z in a harrowing crash on a low-altitude, high-speed run.

Though the Gee Bee R-2 was the aesthetic embodiment of extreme plane designs in the 1930s, it is also the deadliest plane on record: Of the handful of Gee Bees built, almost all of them crashed.

Piper's PA-28 Cherokee features a robust fixed-pitch propeller and sturdy fixed landing gear.

PIPER PA-28 CHEROKEE

Piper introduced the Cherokee—its all-metal, low-wing airplane—in 1960, and it created a bit of a sensation. The PA-28 represented a brand-new business direction: a movement toward entry-level planes very different from and more affordably priced than its iconic J-3 Cub and the later short-wing models Piper built from steel tube and fabric. The leader of the Cherokee's entry-level pack had been the four-seat Tripacer, and it had been a huge market success. So why change styles? Well, the low-wing Cherokee had a modernized look and feel, and it flew great.

The Cherokee's design team included Fred Weick, who fathered the Ercoupe, and John Thorp, developer of an airplane known as the Sky Scooter. Their goal was to modernize the low end of Piper's line, building on the Piper Comanche, a retractable-gear cruiser. They sure delivered, and the Cherokee was given the designation PA-28 to celebrate its place as the twenty-eighth design to come out of Piper Aircraft. It set the stage for the biggest years in Piper's history, inspiring offshoots galore, from the Archer to the Arrow, from the Pathfinder to the Seneca, and it became a remarkably popular trainer plane. Even today, it remains tough to compete with a thirty-year-old Cherokee in terms of quality, price, and cost of operation. Still in limited production, the PA-28 is one of the icons of light aviation.

MESSERSCHMITT BF 109

First introduced in the mid-1930s, the Messerschmitt Bf 109—the plane that was to become the predominant German fighter in World War II—initially struggled to gain governmental support. With an aerodynamically superior, low-wing design and an original max speed of 290 miles per hour (466.75 km/h), however, the all-metal Bf 109 eventually won over its skeptics.

Ironically, the first prototype of the plane flew with a British-built Rolls-Royce Kestrel engine—Rolls-Royce's first inline, cast-block engine—since it was the most advanced of its kind. Willy Messerschmitt wanted an inline engine for its narrow frontal area and low-drag cooling. Retractable landing gear, a narrow fuselage, and an enclosed canopy were more of the design features that gave the stressed-skin fighter its edge.

Like its adversary under development across the English Channel—the Spitfire—the Messerschmitt's landing gear was mounted on the fuselage and retracted outward into the wings. Since the stress of supporting the fighter's weight was not placed on the wing spar, the wing could be narrower for greater speed. The downside to this silhouette was difficult handling on the ground, and more Bf 109s were lost in accidents than fell to Allied guns. While the Fw 190 that entered the war in 1941 surpassed it in performance, the Bf 109's mass production—more than 30,000 were manufactured by the end of the war—cemented its reign as the most famous German fighter of World War II. It was flown by the three top-scoring German fighter aces of the war, who scored 928 victories among them.

The Bf 109's aggressive appearance—it seems to sport a sharklike grimace—may have helped German pilots dominate in combat by intimidating their opponents.

SOPWITH CAMEL

The Sopwith Camel was the most famous British fighter of World War I; many Allied aces amassed their impressive scores while flying one. Originally designed to replace the Sopwith Pup, the Camel carried the unofficial name Big Pup during testing. But that changed when it became the first British pursuit ship (as fighters were known in World War I) to mount a pair of Vickers .303-caliber machine guns that fired through the propeller. The metal covers over the guns' breeches created a hump that led to the name Camel.

When introduced in 1917, the Camel quickly earned a reputation as being difficult to fly. It was powered by a series of rotary engines, which generate tremendous gyroscopic torque due to the fact that all nine heavy cylinders rotate, along with the propeller, around a fixed crankshaft. That made for extra-sharp turns to the right, but very difficult turns to the left. Experienced Allied pilots learned to exploit this quirk in combat, but experienced German pilots learned to expect the Camel to turn right when in a fix.

The Camel also featured sensitive controls and was quick to enter a nasty spin, meaning it needed a skilled pilot to fly it. For example, rotary engines operate at full power or none. So pilots learned to control the plane's engine by connecting and disconnecting the electrical power using a switch. When a Camel came in for a landing, there was a series of on-again, off-again blasts of engine exhaust as the pilot controlled the descent. Still, Camels proved their mettle in combat, shooting down nearly 1,300 enemy airplanes—more than any other Allied fighter of the war.

Today, there's only one genuine Sopwith Camel capable of taking to the skies—occasionally, you can hear it sputtering magnificently above its home in Paso Robles, California.

BEECHCRAFT STAGGERWING

Historically, Beechcraft has made a habit of creating benchmark aircraft designs, including its classic Model 18 Twin Beech, the Bonanza, the Baron light twin, and the King Air twin turboprop. But it was the Model D17 Staggerwing, a fairly early design, that made the greatest impact. In the Staggerwing, Walter Beech created what is arguably the ultimate biplane, with retractable landing gear, a powerful radial engine, and slippery, streamlined aerodynamics—it is possibly the sleekest tube-and-fabric aircraft ever designed.

To achieve the plane's harmonious design, Beech chose the format of a forward lower wing with the top wing staggered to the rear. In the post–Lindbergh Depression era, Beech's mission was clear: Those who had retained their wealth wanted the best, and the pricey Staggerwing was the personal jet of its day, delivering 200-mile-per-hour (321.75-km/h) speed and a luxury cabin on par with the handcrafted limousines coming from custom coachmakers' shops. And in an era when autogiros presaged the future of personal helicopters, the versatile and rugged Staggerwing could take off and land efficiently from a backyard polo field.

Staggerwings went on to become the premier aircraft for the elite, celebrated air racers and versatile warbirds serving on all fronts during World War II. With each model handcrafted to perfection in the Wichita factory that still turns out Beechcraft products, the Staggerwing would also set the standard for one of the most successful manufacturers in history.

The Staggerwing's compact body and snub nose make it look like a dragonfly darting through the sky.

LOCKHEED SR-71 BLACKBIRD

The Mach-3+ SR-71 Blackbird spy plane is hailed as the fastest manned aircraft in history, with the exception of the rocket-powered X-15. Its mission? Fly high and fast enough on its reconnaissance flights to remain out of reach of enemy surface-to-air missiles, and outrun other threats.

The Blackbird became necessary after CIA U-2 reconnaissance plane pilot Francis Gary Powers was shot down over Russia and captured, igniting an international firestorm at the height of the Cold War. After Powers bailed out, his U-2 spy plane landed largely intact and was examined by the Russians. The more advanced SR-71 was conceived by Lockheed's legendary designer Clarence "Kelly" Johnson in the late 1950s to top the U-2 and evade the Russians, and it first flew in 1964 in Area 51, the infamous site of Air Force testing. It entered service two years later and was retired in 1998. By then, much of the high-altitude reconnaissance mission was taken over by surveillance satellites.

A total of thirty-two of the titanium-and-steel Blackbirds were built, and twelve were destroyed in accidents. None was ever lost to enemy fire. SR-71 pilots wore space suits, and their missions regularly took them to the edge of the atmosphere, where the Earth's curvature was clearly visible. *Flying* contributing writer Peter Garrison said of the SR-71, "The Blackbird was leaky, not very maneuverable, and given to cantankerous engine behavior, but it remains possibly the most fantastic-looking—and to many eyes the most beautiful—airplane ever to fly."

"Blackbird" wasn't the SR-71's only nickname: It was also called "Habu" while deployed in Japan, after a Japanese snake it was thought to resemble.

BEECHCRAFT BONANZA

Walter Beech unveiled his all-new V-tail Bonanza just after World War II. Its progeny, the G36, is still in production today, with classic Bonanza performance and flying qualities that keep it at the top of most pilots' wish lists—though the V-tail design was dropped in 1982 due to stronger sales of a straight-tale version. The original Bonanza was revolutionary for the light-plane market of the day. It incorporated innumerable aerodynamic and manufacturing advances that had accelerated during wartime: All-metal monocoque construction (in which the outer casing is integral to the structure), a flat-six-cylinder engine, retractable landing gear, and all-weather instrumentation topped the list.

Most other postwar aircraft manufacturers strove to produce affordable airplanes. But Beech and his wife, Olive Ann, correctly judged that the well-to-do would still desire a more luxurious private aviation experience, and they appointed the Bonanza appropriately for wealthy consumers.

The Bonanza could carry four adults and their luggage in sedanlike comfort at airliner speeds—a mission the company previously had filled with the much more expensive radial-engine Staggerwing, which had more than twice the horsepower of the Bonanza but required more man hours of specialty skilled labor. The Bonanza was the first really modern personal transportation airplane, and it secured Beechcraft's legacy in history. The Bonanza also inspired the Baron, the prototypical twin of the era (a plane that is also still in production today), and the T-34 Mentor, which is considered to be the dominant military trainer of the day.

The Bonanza's unusual butterfly V-tail was designed to make the plane lighter and aerodynamically cleaner than a conventional tail.

BOEING B-52 STRATOFORTRESS

Initially designed as a high-altitude strategic bomber in the 1940s, the Boeing B-52 Stratofortress has endured decades of changing threats and demands, remaining in operational use for more than fifty years—more than half the total history of manned flight. With a range of more than 10,000 miles (16,093.5 km), an altitude capability greater than 50,000 feet (15,240 m), and a bomb payload of approximately 70,000 pounds (31.75 mt), the B-52 was built to be a bastion of deterrence during the Cold War. But the plane's role expanded over time to include various roles, like low-altitude bombing, reconnaissance, and combat support, just to name a few.

The B-52 was designed to carry nuclear bombs, but it never has during combat: Although it flew combat missions during several wars, it only ever dropped conventional bombs. It did drop thermonuclear weapons during tests that were conducted at Bikini Atoll in the South Pacific, however.

The B-52's family tree includes the Boeing B-17 Flying Fortress and the B-29 Superfortress, both piston-powered bombers from World War II. The original 1946 design mandate called for a straight-wing, six-engine turboprop, but the direction of the project soon led to a swept-wing pure jet with eight engines mounted on four underwing pylons.

The official name of the B-52 is Stratofortress. But because it has never been known as one of the prettiest aircraft to hit the skies, its most commonly used nickname is the "BUFF"—an acronym which, in its family-friendly version, stands for "Big Ugly Fat . . . Fella."

During its lengthy history, the eight-engine, swept-wing B-52 has shattered speed and range records, and it remains a key player in contemporary U.S. military operations.

CESSNA 208 CARAVAN

With the carrying capability of the Caravan, it shouldn't come as a surprise that FedEx contributed ideas to the design: In aviation's lean years during the 1980s, Cessna's primary manufacturing capacity was focused on building Caravans for the package-delivery giant. Dispatch reliability was of primary concern for FedEx, so the 208 was equipped with a tried-and-true Pratt & Whitney PT6 turboprop engine producing 600 horsepower (later upgraded to 675 horsepower). Also on FedEx's agenda was the goal of developing a docile airplane that could be flown under a variety of weather conditions, even by less-experienced pilots.

With its familiar strutted wing design and fixed landing gear, the Caravan has been called "a 182 on steroids"—182 referring to Cessna's well-loved personal transportation cruiser. The result of mating the turboprop engine with a flying van of an airplane ended up paying off: It turned out to be a match made in heavy-hauling heaven.

But as well as the Caravan fulfilled the FedEx mission, it was good for other things, too: *Versatility* is probably the word that describes the big Cessna turboprop best. The airplane can be equipped with an extra cargo pod and multiple types of landing gear, including bush tires, amphibious floats, and skis. It is also available with an executive interior rivaling the amenities of business jets costing big bucks. Excellent short takeoff-and-landing capabilities allow this reasonably large airplane to get in and out of tight backcountry airstrips, too.

The short-body Caravan is a popular model to put on amphibious floats, an option that allows owners to take the big single just about anywhere their hearts desire.

ROBINSON R22

Designing a practical light helicopter has significant challenges, but after working for several helicopter manufacturers including Cessna, Bell, and Hughes, Frank Robinson saw an opportunity to launch his own light design. Among the hurdles he faced was the need to ensure sufficient cooling airflow for a piston engine. He also needed to develop a rotor system that was robust yet light enough to perform well with the low power output his light craft would require.

After six years of development, Robinson Helicopters introduced the R22, which received FAA certification in 1979. Power from the 150-horsepower engine is transferred to the main and tail rotors via a system of V-belts. The rotor blades have relatively low inertia, making the controls light and sensitive. Pilots who train on R22s have little trouble transitioning to heavier helicopters with higher-inertia rotor systems for greater stability in flight, especially in hover.

With a reasonable purchase price and low operating cost, the two-seat, two-blade design became a huge success, enabling Robinson to expand his company's product offering. The four-seat R44 followed, and then the R66 turbine-powered variant. Robinsons are used in many roles, including training, sightseeing, law enforcement, pipeline and wildlife patrol, electronic news gathering, and just plain fun flying. Thirty-two years after the R22 was introduced, more than 10,000 Robinson helicopters have been delivered out of the ever-expanding factory in Torrance, California.

Popular as a trainer, the rugged, reliable Robinson R22 is low in cost and operational expenses, bringing the dream of helicopter flying within reach of a wide range of pilots.

BOEING 737

When Boeing introduced the 737 to service in 1968, no one expected it to become the iconic jet transport that it has: More "Seven-Threes" have been built than any other airliner ever—even more than Douglas's piston DC-3 airliner, which was built by the thousands during World War II.

The Boeing 737 was initially conceived to be the narrow-body, twin-engine replacement for the company's aging, fuel-thirsty tri-jet 727. Germany's Lufthansa was the launch customer, ordering twenty-one planes in 1965 at a price of U.S.$3.2 million each. United Airlines followed with an order for forty, but asked for more capacity. Boeing stretched the fuselage a total of 76 inches

(193 cm), and the resulting variant was given the 200 suffix. Today, there are numerous variants, including one with a capacity of as many as 215 passengers. Counting all models, close to 7,500 have been delivered to date, and more than 3,000 are still on order, awaiting their turn on the crowded assembly line.

Modern improvements to the 737 include flat-panel avionics, winglets (wingtip extensions that reduce drag), and extended range. One variant, the Boeing Business Jet, comes with bedroom suites and showers. The current production model is the 900 series, with a newly reengineered 737-MAX slated to enter service in 2017, half a century after the first flight of the original 737-100.

Boeing's 737 was initially designed as a short-range flier. As it happened, the 737 has become the most prolific airliner ever built: At any given time, there are 1,250 737s airborne throughout the world. Two are taking off or landing every five seconds.

LOCKHEED P-38 LIGHTNING

The P-38 Lightning was one of only two American fighters in service throughout all of the United States' involvement in World War II, from Pearl Harbor to Victory-over-Japan Day. Though the sleek single-seater's distinctive twin-boom tails led rival pilots of the German Luftwaffe to nickname it the "Fork-Tailed Devil," most American fighter pilots had no experience in multiengine planes—and many were leery of the P-38. But a talented young lieutenant named Bob Hoover was assigned to travel among fighter bases demonstrating its performance and showing the pilots they had nothing to fear.

In fact, the plane's second engine allowed many a grateful Lightning pilot to make it home after one of his engines had been damaged by enemy fire. The P-38 scored its biggest victories in the Pacific and was the primary long-range fighter of the Army Air Forces until the P-51 Mustang started arriving in large numbers toward the end of the war. Famously, Major Richard Bong, America's highest scoring "ace of aces"—with forty confirmed Japanese planes destroyed—flew a P-38 with a portrait of his wife, Marge, painted on the nose.

Designed by Lockheed engineer Clarence "Kelly" Johnson and his team, the P-38 represented one of the most radical departures in the history of American fighter development. The Lightning was a complete breakaway from conventional designs, yet its odd looks yielded the power of two engines and, at long last, the ability to carry heavy armament.

The distinctive twin-boom configuration of the P-38 was both a blessing and a curse: It was easily identifiable by enemy fighters, but the second engine brought home many a P-38 pilot after sustaining battle damage.

BLÉRIOT XI

In the early twentieth century, the English Channel seemed as profound a barrier for early aeronauts as the Atlantic Ocean was for Lindbergh twenty years later. In 1909, an intrepid Frenchman, Louis Blériot, became the first to fly the Channel, opening the eyes of Europeans to the enthralling potential of this new phenomenon—the aeroplane. His Blériot XI was a wood-framed monoplane with a bathtublike cockpit. Its 25-horsepower, three-cylinder Anzani engine was mounted up front, balanced by tail feathers offset well aft of the cockpit. Blériot's configuration was quite unlike the *Wright Flyer*, a strutted biplane with a mid-engine and forward-mounted control surfaces. And Blériot's version eventually became the standard due to its efficiency and stability.

Blériot's Channel crossing took a mere thirty-six minutes but forever changed the relationship between England and the countries of the European continent. Blériot was so smitten with his design that he chose to mass-produce it—and he did a fine job of it, because today, a century later, the oldest flyable airplane in the world is a Blériot XI, operated by the Shuttleworth Collection at Old Warden Aerodrome in the United Kingdom. Believed to have been built just a few weeks later, the second oldest plane is the Blériot XI with serial number 56. This one is the oldest flyable airplane in the Western hemisphere, and still makes crow-hop flights down a grass runway on calm days at the Old Rhinebeck Aerodrome flying museum in Rhinebeck, New York.

When it crossed the English Channel in 1909, Louis Blériot's Model XI provided a look into the future, offering a glimpse at just how small air travel could make the world. In England, the headline in the next day's *The Daily Express* read "Britain is no longer an island."

HINDENBURG

Fine china and excellent service were among the amenities enjoyed by passengers on the early airships that traveled the world in the 1930s. In the era before heavier-than-air technology could go the distance, these slow, majestic airships represented the ultimate in high-tech transportation: Modeled after ocean liners, their passenger cabins were an absolute study in luxurious splendor.

At 803¾ feet (245 m) long—just 78 feet (23.75 m) shorter than the *Titanic*—Germany's *Hindenburg*, LZ 129, holds the record as the largest aircraft ever to take to the air, despite the fact that it's been more than seven decades since its maiden flight in 1936. Built on the success of its predecessor, the Graf Zeppelin, the *Hindenburg* held more than 7 million cubic feet (198,218 m³)

of hydrogen and could produce double its own weight in tons of gross lift. The *Hindenburg* was originally designed to use helium, but the United States refused to yield its monopoly to Nazi Germany, so the zeppelin used hydrogen instead.

This great aircraft carried more than 2,500 passengers across the Atlantic before it burst into flames while landing in Lakehurst, New Jersey, in 1937, killing thirty-six people. Tests conducted in 2013 suggest that the crash may have been caused by static electricity, though sabotage and lightning have long been rumored as possible causes. The crash, recorded on newsreels and punctuated by live radio broadcaster Herbert Morrison's anguished eyewitness report, hastened the conclusion to the brief era of passenger airship travel.

The *Hindenburg* was a rigid airship: Its structure was made up of an aluminum frame filled with sixteen cotton gas bags holding the lift-giving hydrogen gas. The entire structure was covered in treated fabric.

BAe Harriers have been operated by several countries around the world, including the United States, Britain, Italy, and Spain.

BAE HARRIER

As the first successful strike fighter able to perform vertical landings, the latest variants of the BAe Harrier jet brought a slew of revolutionary capabilities to the forefront of Western air defense. The mission of the Harrier's creators was to design a combat aircraft that could not only perform effectively in high-speed attack mode but also land and take off from a space no larger than a parking lot or forest clearing.

The aircraft was a product of both American and British innovation and, like earlier Harrier jets, relies on thrust vectoring technology for its wide range of vertical and horizontal maneuverability: Vanes at the engines' outlets are movable and can direct the thrust either straight down for hovering or out the back for high-speed forward flight. With

that maneuverability, a more powerful engine, an airframe composed substantially of composites, and more payload capacity, the BAe Harrier emerged as a multidimensional fighter.

On the air-show circuit, the BAe Harrier is loud, fast, and impressive when slowed to hover mode in front of a crowd. During a show, talented demonstration pilots sometimes "bow" the plane to onlookers and fans. Carrying on the vertical takeoff and landing capability of the Harrier, its planned replacement is a version of Lockheed Martin's F-35B Lightning II with the same thrust vectoring technology. The F-35 is scheduled to enter service with the U.S. Marine Corp and the Italian Navy starting in 2014, but there's no doubt that the Harrier will continue to thrill crowds.

HEROES OF AVIATION

From the first crow hops into the air to rocket voyages to the surface of the moon, pilots have exhibited their courage. They have also shown that humans can adapt their instincts and intuition to a new element—with movement in three dimensions rather than two. Today, with the growing role of remotely piloted drones, some question whether airplanes need pilots anymore. But even with all the automation, there will always be situations involving rogue weather, bird strikes, or equipment malfunctions that demonstrate the lifesaving worth of humans flying "by the seat of their pants."

1911

Calbraith Perry Rodgers

One of aviation's largely unsung heroes, Calbraith Perry Rodgers struck out from New York on September 17, 1911, trying to be the first to fly from coast to coast. He had received ninety minutes of instruction from Orville Wright forty-one days earlier. Sponsored by the Armour company, his aircraft was an early model made by the Wright brothers and named *Vin Fiz* for one of the company's products, a soft drink. Perry finally arrived at Long Beach, California, on November 5 after seventy stops along the way, many after crash landings. Rodgers died after a crash several months later when he collided with a flock of birds during a demonstration—aviation's first fatality from a bird strike.

1929

Jimmy Doolittle

Best known for leading the 1942 B-25 raid on Tokyo from the aircraft carrier USS *Hornet,* Jimmy Doolittle had already achieved fame—first as a daredevil race pilot, winning the Schneider Trophy in 1925, and then for the first "blind flight" (taking off and landing solely by reference to his instruments) on September 25, 1929. He went on to serve as a general in the Army Air Forces during World War II.

1937

Amelia Earhart

Aviation's most legendary female pilot, Earhart took her first exhilarating trip to the skies for U.S.$10 in 1920. From that excursion, Earhart knew she had to fly herself and saved for her first plane: a Kinner Airster biplane, dubbed the *Canary*. She was the first woman and the second person to fly solo across the Atlantic (earning the first Flying Cross given to a woman) and the first person to fly alone across the Pacific from Honolulu to California. Tragically, in an effort to win the title of the first person to circumnavigate the globe at the Equator, Earhart's Lockheed Electra disappeared into the Pacific Ocean in 1937. But her legacy is still a source of intrigue and inspiration.

1927

Charles Lindbergh

As an airmail pilot flying obsolete crates, Charles Lindbergh daydreamed of a modern ship with enough gas to just keep on flying all the way to Paris. Perhaps his greatest talent was in convincing backers that he could actually do it. His successful solo flight from New York to Paris in May 1927 in the *Spirit of St. Louis* ignited a media firestorm the likes of which had never been seen before—and hasn't been duplicated since. One of the results: an enduring aviation magazine founded in 1927, known today as *Flying*.

1940

Douglas Bader

RAF wing commander Douglas "Tin Legs" Bader lost both legs in a flying accident in 1931, but managed to bluster his way back into active service in time for the Battle of Britain in 1940. While leading combat missions, he once astounded his fellow pilots by demanding over the radio that fighter control call up his squash partner and tell him that he would be late for his game due to an inconvenient intrusion by the Luftwaffe. Downed over France in 1941, Bader was taken prisoner and made four escape attempts. Knighted in 1976, his accomplishments during and after the war remain an inspiration for amputees to this day.

1947

Charles "Chuck" Yeager

Already a hero combat pilot, West Virginian Charles "Chuck" Yeager could have rested on his wartime laurels. Instead, he sought out the most dangerous postwar duty as an experimental test pilot in the new Air Force jet program. Though he lacked a formal education, Yeager's abilities as an aviator and his intuitive engineering skills made him first choice to pilot the Bell X-1 rocket plane in its quest to exceed Mach 1. The first to break the sound barrier—and survive—his successful flight is legendary. And it's been theorized that all pilots imitate Chuck Yeager's drawl over the radio.

1969

Neil Armstrong

When asked what it was like to walk on the moon, Neil Armstrong once answered, "You'd like it." A shy and humble man, he made history as the first human to look back at Earth from the solid ground of another heavenly body. He took that "one small step for a man" on July 20, 1969, answering President John Kennedy's May 25, 1961, challenge to reach the moon by the end of the decade. Neil Armstrong died in 2012, leaving behind a legacy unsurpassed by any of aviation's greatest achievements, before or since.

1979

R. A. "Bob" Hoover

"The pilots' pilot," Robert A. "Bob" Hoover is best known for his air-show routine, flying the twin-engine Aero Commander Shrike with one or both engines shut down. Hoover got his start doing demonstrations for military pilots in Lockheed P-38 Lightnings during World War II, in which he was taken as a prisoner of war but bravely escaped by flying a liberated Fw-190 into Holland. He was Chuck Yeager's backup for the Bell X-1 flight that broke the sound barrier in 1947, and he later served as a top civilian test pilot in the development of supersonic jet fighters. As renowned as he is for his flying skill, Hoover is equally regarded as a showman, an ambassador for aviation, and one of the true gentlemen of the industry.

1944

Benjamin O. Davis, Jr.

During the buildup to World War II, when the U.S. Army desperately needed pilots, U.S. military culture still discriminated against African-American pilots. The success in combat of the Red Tails, led by Benjamin Davis, was a key step in advancing equality in the U.S. military. Davis was the first black officer to solo an Army Air Corps airplane, and he was appointed commanding officer of the 332 Fighter Group. He completed sixty combat missions in Europe, flew jet fighters in Korea, and ended his career as a four-star general.

1958

Alvin "Tex" Johnston

Boeing test pilot Alvin "Tex" Johnston decided to impress an international airline group by barrel-rolling the manufacturer's four-engine 707 jetliner prototype over Seattle. A flight engineer snapped a telltale picture from the cabin of the airplane, and a legend was born. When he explained to the president of Boeing that the 1-G maneuver was completely safe, the boss responded, "You know that. Now we know that. But just don't do it anymore." Johnston also helped design and fly the Bell X-1, was the first person to fly the B-52, and moved into the Space Age by managing both the Saturn and Apollo programs with NASA.

2009

Chesley "Sully" Sullenberger

With their emergency landing on New York's Hudson River in January 2009, US Airways captain Chesley "Sully" Sullenberger and copilot Jeffrey Skiles proved that, even with all the automation that makes airline flying routine, there are still situations where pilot skill and sangfroid can work wonders. After a devastating collision with a flock of large geese, Flight 1549's Airbus A320 lost all engine power just after takeoff from LaGuardia Airport. With all other options eliminated, Sullenberger told controllers, "We're going to be in the Hudson." Everyone on board survived.

CESSNA CITATION X

First introduced in 1996, Cessna's Citation X (named for the roman numeral 10) set the pace as the world's fastest business jet—and became the fastest civilian airplane when the Concorde fleet was retired in 2003. In 2010, Cessna updated its program, and the result is the new Citation X. It reclaims the title as the world's fastest civilian airplane, which the previous model briefly surrendered to the slightly faster Gulfstream G650 in 2012.

The X's computer-controlled Rolls-Royce engines are enormous, making it look like the hot-rod jet that it is. But even going back to when the original X first hit the market, it's always been about a lot more than just speed.

The cabin interior, though not roomy, ensures comfort and a productive work environment while en route. And the new Citation X has stretched that cabin farther for a bit more space. Upgraded Rolls-Royce AE3007C2 engines produce more thrust and improved specific fuel consumption for more speed, yet lower fuel burn and increased range. Energy-saving winglets are now standard, ensuring even greater fuel efficiency and climb capability.

The new Citation X is also the launch customer for Garmin's G5000 touch-screen avionics suite, which includes computerized synthetic vision. The Citation X earned Cessna the prestigious Collier Trophy in 1996.

The raw power of the Citation X is evident from the oversize engine nacelles. Steeply swept wings and tail help make it look fast even when standing still. At 37 degrees, the wing sweep is the sharpest on any business jet, contrasting with the unswept wings of many of its siblings in the Citation line.

LUSCOMBE MODEL 8 SILVAIRE

With most light airplanes using traditional steel-tube and fabric construction, Donald Luscombe's all-metal Model 8 Silvaire was at least a bit revolutionary. The company motto—"No wood, no nails, no glue"—boasted of the advanced technology incorporated for the first time in such a light airplane. First produced in the late 1930s, the Silvaire made its mark on the light aircraft scene with this monocoque design, which endowed the Luscombe with speeds 10 to 20 miles per hour (16–32 km/h) faster than its similarly powered competition. The original Model 8 was equipped with a fabric-covered wing, but later, more prolific versions of the aircraft traded in the fabric for aluminum material. And though the original had a 50-horsepower Continental A-50 flat-four engine, later derivatives swapped out the A-50 for more powerful engines, such as the A-65 and the 90-horsepower C-90.

As part of his business plan, Don Luscombe established the Luscombe School of Aeronautics to teach aircraft manufacturing and maintenance at his factory in Trenton, New Jersey. He tapped many of his students as production workers, but none seemed to mind, as he also housed and fed many of them in a sort of aero-commune family.

Thanks to its responsive controls, the high-wing two-seater has garnered a reputation as an aircraft that demands an acute touch from a proficient pilot, a reputation that has endured throughout the decades along with the Luscombe's appeal among classic aircraft enthusiasts.

Luscombe Model 8 Silvaires are well loved for their simple, light, all-metal design. Faster than most of the other low-powered "flivvers" of the 1930s, they enjoyed strong sales among personal fliers.

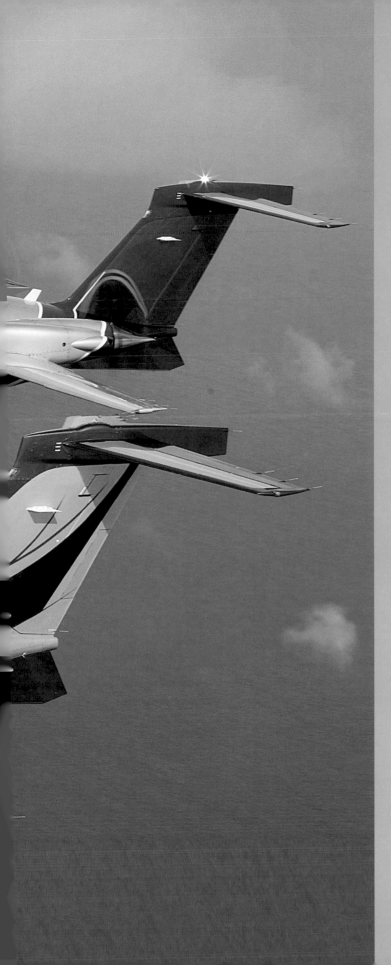

PIAGGIO AERO P.180 AVANTI

It's impossible to mistake this airplane for any other, whether it's up close on the tarmac or high above—even before you see it, the distinctive sound of its twin-pusher propellers lets you know there's a Piaggio Aero P.180 Avanti in the neighborhood. This uniquely configured turboprop twin started as a collaboration between Piaggio of Italy and Learjet in America; their aim was to design and produce a sleek, modern turboprop capable of challenging the Beech King Air, and even business jets, in performance and comfort. Learjet dropped out of the program in early 1986, but Piaggio forged ahead, flying the prototype nine months later.

Although U.S. and European certification was obtained in 1990, the project languished for the next eight years due to funding woes and, probably, buyer apprehension due to the Avanti's odd looks. But the aft-facing engines and propellers that give the plane its unique silhouette also make for a quieter cabin environment, leaving all the noise in the plane's slipstream. Plus, the Avanti's speed and economical fuel burn make it a winner against almost any competitor, and comparable to aircraft costing much more.

In 1998, a group of investors led by Piero Ferrari (yes, that Ferrari) became involved. By then the Avanti had proven its capabilities, and sales soon followed. In 2005, the Avanti II earned its certification and, with its updated PT6A engines and modern Rockwell Collins avionics, was an immediate hit. Piaggio has produced more than two hundred, and sales have remained strong.

With its short forward wings, pusher propellers, downward-sloping tail surface, and landing gear that extends from its belly, the Piaggio Avanti sports a distinctive and unusual shape.

FORD TRI-MOTOR

In the early 1920s, the ambitious aircraft designer William Stout explored the use of aluminum alloy. His aptly named Stout Metal Airplane Company was shortly thereafter bought by Henry Ford, hoping to do for the budding aviation industry what he had accomplished for the automotive world. Stout's original design had been a single-engine airplane—but under Ford, it was redesigned with three 200-horsepower Wright J4 radial engines and later produced with more robust Pratt & Whitney Wasps.

In the Roaring '20s, an age of wood- or steel-tube airplanes covered in fabric, the all-metal Ford stood out as a technological leap forward.

Its corrugated aluminum skin (for added strength) led to nicknames such as "Flying Washboard" and "Tin Goose."

All jokes aside, the gleaming, metallic aircraft proved rugged, reasonably priced, and highly reliable. Its stellar performance in its air-transport role helped grow the public's faith in safe air travel, and it quickly became America's most popular airline platform. The Tri-Motor later proved its worth and resilience in a variety of other uses, such as cargo and military transport. Several examples of the Ford Tri-Motor are still flying, so it's possible to experience the early feel of flying as an airline passenger firsthand.

The Ford Tri-Motor is easily distinguished by its corrugated aluminum skin. It made quite an impact on the world of personal travel; Franklin Roosevelt even traveled on one during his 1932 campaign.

143

NORTH AMERICAN P-51 MUSTANG

In 1940, while Britain was under siege from the German Luftwaffe, the country asked North American Aviation to build Curtiss P-40s for it under license. The company replied, "Give us a little time, and we'll give you something much better." Combining government data on laminar-flow wings—which allowed the smooth, uninterrupted flow of air over an airplane's wings—with the most up-to-date research on aerodynamic engine cooling, North American rolled out what is widely considered to be the best piston-engine fighter ever built—the P-51 Mustang—117 days later.

Soon paired with the British Spitfire's Rolls-Royce Merlin engine, the Mustang became an instant hit with American fighter pilots because of its nimble handling, high-altitude capabilities, and fast speeds. Best of all, its efficiency and fuel capacity allowed the Mustang to save countless aircrew lives. Aviation legend Bob Hoover said, "The Rolls-Royce engine made it a tremendously different airplane [compared with the original non-supercharged Allison engine]. It gave it the ability to fight all the way up to 40,000 feet [12,192 m] and defend the bombers from the time they got over enemy territory until they returned to friendly territory. It was the first airplane capable of doing that."

The Mustang was also designed to be easily mass produced, an attribute that contributed to its deployment in more than fifty countries worldwide. More than 15,000 Mustangs have been built, and around 180 of those—having been lovingly restored and maintained—are still flying, giving today's air-show crowds a glimpse into the past glories of World War II's Greatest Generation.

Mustang pilots shot down more than 4,900 enemy aircraft in World War II, a total that was surpassed only by the Grumman F6F Hellcat among Allied aircraft.

HAWKER SIDDELEY HS-125

The Hawker Siddeley HS-125 began life as the de Havilland DH125; passed through numerous corporate mergers, acquisitions, and name changes; and wound up on an assembly line in Wichita, Kansas. The prototype took flight in 1962. It was, according to some, the first official production business jet to take to the skies (some attribute that honor to America's four-engine Lockheed JetStar, but others point out that the JetStar was first built for a military contract proposal). Through the years, the basic design of the 125 has been modified, upgraded, and refined, and today, most in the industry know it simply as the "Hawker."

Initially powered by twin 3,000-pound (1,360.75-mt) thrust Viper turbojet engines, the revolutionary aircraft was slightly slower than its competitors but more than made up for its relative lack of speed with cabin comfort and economy. Those attributes helped lay the foundation for it to become one of the top-selling bizjet lines in history. The Hawker line survived into the new millennium before it was discontinued in 2013, and the modern models that rolled off Hawker Beechcraft's Wichita assembly lines were based on the same 125 airframe that was established during the administration of John F. Kennedy. Its endurance is a testament to the jet's brilliant original design.

Known by many corporate names during its half century of production, the Hawker line of business jets (one is shown here with its landing gear in transition) evolved into a modern, long-range midsize jet from its origin as one of the first of the breed.

SPACE SHUTTLE

According to astronaut and space shuttle pilot Robert "Hoot" Gibson, "The space shuttle must go down in history as the most revolutionary advancement in aviation ever." He makes a strong case—it's true that flight at hypersonic speeds in an operational aircraft had never been accomplished before the space shuttle took its first revolutionary flight in 1982.

It had taken decades to get to that first flight: The goal of developing a reusable low-orbit spacecraft (which orbits primarily within the Earth's atmosphere) like the shuttle was conceived of in 1969, the same year Neil Armstrong walked on the Moon, but budget cuts delayed the program for more than a decade. Eventually, five orbiters were built. Powered by solid boosters and engines that burned liquid oxygen and hydrogen and provided 7.5 million pounds (3,402 mt) of thrust, the space shuttle was able to loft more than a stunning 30,000 pounds (13.5 mt) of cargo into orbit.

Its roles were various and significant: It rescued satellites, helped build the International Space Station, and launched the Hubble Telescope. In all, the five orbiters flew a total of 135 missions. The program suffered two tragic accidents, in which the crews of the *Challenger* (1986) and the *Columbia* (2003) were lost. Space shuttle *Atlantis* launched on the aircraft's final mission on July 8, 2011, landing at the Kennedy Space Center in Florida at dawn on July 21.

The space shuttle typically orbited the Earth at an altitude between 200 miles (322 km) and 400 miles (643.75 km).

CIRRUS SR22

The dream of brothers Alan and Dale Klapmeier, the four-seat, all-composite Cirrus SR22 was a higher-powered planned upgrade of the highly successful SR20, which remains in production. The company prides itself on innovation, and with the SR22, it delivered in spades. The SR22 was the first all-composite general aviation plane produced in any numbers. Ironically, one of that plane's most prominent features is that it does not have retractable landing gear, which was previously considered a staple step-up for any high-performance airplane. Cirrus determined that the drag reduction of retractable gear was not worth the extra weight and complexity, and that made insurance companies happier, too, as they didn't have to worry about expensive gear-up landings.

With aerodynamically shaped wheel covers and struts, the fixed-gear SR22 has plenty of speed. Of special note is the airplane's revolutionary whole-airplane recovery parachute system, which has saved dozens of lives to date. It also features a spin-resistant wing design, a side-yoke controller (an alternative to a control grip that's sometimes shaped like a U), lots of room, and lots of glass.

Though original models came with the standard setup of a half-dozen mechanically driven instruments in the panel, Cirrus continued its innovation by being the first to offer computerized flat-panel avionics, later adding enhanced vision, envelope protection (preventing a pilot from exceeding performance limits), a terrain-alert system, traffic information, electronic chart databases, and more. The SR22 gave pilots of light airplanes most of the same advantages that corporate and airline jet pilots had enjoyed for years. Today there are more than 5,000 Cirrus aircraft in the field.

One of general aviation's great success stories, Cirrus continues to innovate the SR-22, making private flying a safer and more dependable form of personal transportation for its customers.

BEDE BD-5

One can tell by looking that the Bede BD-5 has a unique and impressive airplane design. Its mastermind, Jim Bede, had established his presence as a home-built airplane designer with four models before producing the BD-5. In fact, the BD-1 evolved into the Grumman American AA1 series of light trainers, albeit long after Bede had passed the design on to others. Bede's fifth creation was a tiny single-seater with the engine mounted behind the pilot, who sat under a glass canopy like a jet fighter pilot. The combination of the plane's miniature-fighter silhouette and its relatively affordable price made it seem destined to be a hit.

Unfortunately, in addition to clever design, the BD-5's legacy exemplifies the failed promotion of a kit program. Jim Bede was convinced he had a game-changing airplane in the BD-5 and began taking deposits not only for plans and kits (more than 5,000) but also a reported 12,000 U.S.$600

deposits for a factory-built version he was sure would be approved by the FAA. Bede saw his deposit-holders as risk-sharing partners in his enterprise. But when it all went wrong, they saw themselves as scammed consumers.

The company went bankrupt in the mid-1970s after only a few hundred kits were completed. Of those few hundred, though, were a number of jet-powered versions, some of which went on to succeed on the air-show circuit. A BD-5 jet was even featured in the James Bond film, *Octopussy*, flying through an open hangar.

Today, the BD-5 is remembered for its dizzying speed, brazen acrobatic abilities, and incredibly light fiberglass and aluminum frame—the BD-5J variant weighs in at a world-record-breaking 358¾ pounds (162.75 kg). Several companies have sprung up to supply improved kits and parts to pilots who have the Bede bug, and an estimated thirty aircraft still fly today.

With a compact form reminiscent of a mini rocket ship and a fighterlike cockpit, the BD-5 captured the imagination of potential aircraft kit builders in the early 1970s.

In April 1944, Howard Hughes and TWA president Jack Frye flew from Burbank, California, to Washington, D.C., in a Connie, stopping in Ohio to give Orville Wright a ride. It turned out to be the last airplane ride of Orville's life.

LOCKHEED CONSTELLATION

The legendary "Connie" has to be one of the prettiest planes ever conceived: With its sinuously curving fuselage, triple tail, and tapered wing, it is instantly recognizable. The details of its conception and production, however, are hazy.

In 1939, Trans World Airlines asked Lockheed for a forty-passenger transcontinental airliner with a top speed higher than 340 miles per hour (547 km/h)—that was faster than the superfast Japanese Zero fighter. History states that legendary figure Howard Hughes designed the resulting Constellation, but Hughes's role in the design and acquisition of the plane by TWA, like much of the history of the enigmatic entrepreneur, is a controversial topic today. Some

maintain that Jack Frye, president of TWA at the time, should get more credit than Hughes.

But both sides of the controversy agree that Hughes fully backed the investment in the new airplane, and that it would not have been successful without him. It wasn't until after flying over the Hump during World War II that the Constellation came into its own as a fast, long-haul transport airplane. Lockheed built more than 850 of the aircraft, with the Connie and later the Super Connie ruling the skies until turbojet airliners arrived in the 1950s. Several examples survive, but only two Connies are still in airworthy condition.

ECLIPSE 500

One of the most fascinating stories in all of aviation is that of the Eclipse 500 jet, the private pilot's ultimate dream. When work on the plane began in 2001, the Eclipse was the tip of the spear of the anticipated "very light jet" class, which was expected to change the face of air transport. Perhaps the biggest hope—held by computer guru and unabashed aviation enthusiast Vern Raburn, who headed the Eclipse's development—was that VLJs would spawn a pervasive air-taxi industry, making every small airport a gateway to easy, cheap jet transportation. With six seats and weighing in at a mere 5,950 pounds (2.75 mt), but with a maximum certified altitude of 41,000 feet (12,496.75 m), the Eclipse seemed too good to be true.

Unfortunately, the airplane's creation and promotion took years, cost a billion dollars, and left hundreds of would-be owners out hundreds of thousands each.

In one of the biggest blows, cruise missile engineer pioneer Dr. Sam Williams designed an engine core with all the accessories mounted on the airframe, but sadly it was never able to deliver the power needed, and Raburn shifted to a more conventional engine configuration from Pratt & Whitney Canada in 2004. The program was further plagued by trouble with the plane's avionics and engine controls, and a flawed certification process attracted unwanted attention to the jet.

After all was said and done, Eclipse went bankrupt, but the airplane—which was heralded by pilots for its safety, quiet performance, and smooth handling—survived. Eclipse Aviation took over its production and earned a production certificate for the Eclipse jet, and the new Eclipse (dubbed the Eclipse 550) now does everything Raburn always said it would.

The Eclipse 500 was a six-seater with an all-metal structure, straight wings, and a T-tail. At the time of its introduction, it was the only general aviation jet on the market without a lavatory.

BOEING B-29 SUPERFORTRESS

The largest and most advanced bomber of its day, Boeing's B-29 Superfortress brought a variety of new technologies to American forces during World War II. Powered by four eighteen-cylinder Wright R-3350 engines, the heavy strategic bomber boasted a 20,000-pound (9-mt) bomb load, a top speed of 365 miles per hour (587.5 km/h), and a range of 6,000 miles (9,656 km). In addition, the Superfortress was the first to offer its crew members pressurized compartments, as well as remote-controlled gun turrets. Evolved from the Boeing B-17 Flying Fortress, the B-29 saw its first order from the Army Air Corps in May 1941, about six months before the attack on Pearl Harbor.

First envisioned as a high-altitude, high-speed bomber designed to attack the Japanese homeland, the Superfortress was eventually used primarily for relatively low-level firebombing of Japanese cities. Of course, the B-29's most lasting legacy was its nuclear capability—a power implemented during the atomic bombing of Hiroshima and Nagasaki, events followed by the Japanese surrender. After the war ended, most World War II–era bombers were retired, but the B-29 continued to serve in various roles throughout the 1950s. The British Royal Air Force flew the B-29 (renamed as Washington), and some were even repurposed as flying television transmitters.

The Commemorative Air Force, based in Texas, operates the sole remaining flying example of the B-29. The airframe was rescued from an aircraft boneyard, restored to flying status, and christened *Fifi*. Keeping *Fifi* airworthy is a full-time job, and fueling those four thirsty engines is mighty expensive.

SPAD S.XIII

French manufacturer Société Pour l'Aviation et ses Dérivés (SPAD) was led by famous airplane maker Louis Blériot. He took over SPAD—first named Société de Production des Aéroplanes Deperdussin—following its bankruptcy and the fraud conviction of founder Armand Deperdussin, and the new enterprise developed several World War I fighter models. The most successful among them was the S.XIII biplane. Designed by Louis Béchereau, one of the pioneers of the monocoque fuselage design, the S.XIII first flew in 1917. In the space of a few years during the Great War, aviation technology made enormous strides, leapfrogging from spindly, underpowered ships barely capable of sustained flight to sleek, robust designs with more than double the horsepower, thanks to stronger, more reliable engines.

The SPAD was equipped with the Hispano-Suiza V-8 engine, which developed up to 220 horsepower—twice that of the LeRhone rotary engines found on the French Nieuports and British Sopwith Camels that hit the market just months before the S.XIII. Besides providing greater speed, the more powerful engine also translated to less need for lift-inducing wings. Thus the SPAD featured relatively short wings, increasing its roll rate and, therefore, its turn radius. In combat, the ability to turn on a dime was a game changer—and it was one of the S.XIII's qualities that fighter pilots such as legendary World War I ace Eddie Rickenbacker appreciated. No wonder so many S.XIIIs were ordered: 8,472 were built during the war, and orders for another 10,000 had to be canceled upon the Armistice.

The SPAD S.XIII represented the pinnacle of World War I aviation technology. Several famous Allied fighter pilots earned accolades from its cockpit, including Italian Francesco Baracca and French aces Georges Guynemer and René Fonck.

BOEING 747

With a tail the height of a six-story building and a wing area bigger than a basketball court, the Boeing 747 truly earned its keep as the world's first jumbo jet. Despite its whopping 875,000-pound (397-mt) maximum takeoff weight, the 747's four Pratt & Whitney JT9D-3 engines each provide 43,000 pounds (19.5 mt) of thrust, which gives the aircraft a long range of 6,000 miles (9,656 km) and a speed of up to 570 miles per hour (917.25 km/h). Initially flown by Pan Am in 1970, the 747 held the top spot in terms of passenger capacity for nearly forty years. Even the distinctive humpback of the plane's roomy fuselage—initially meant to accommodate a lounge—was given over to additional seats. Some joked that the raised roof allowed the captain to sit on his wallet.

Interestingly, Boeing designed the 747 to be easily converted into a cargo carrier, since the company believed that the next generation of airliners would all be supersonic—reducing the 747, and all other subsonic airliners, to the role of box haulers. That it drew these assumptions is not surprising, since the initial concept of the 747 grew from a preliminary request from the U.S. Air Force for a heavy-lift cargo plane. Nevertheless, the craft found its true calling as a passenger jet and has been indispensable in that role. It's logged enough miles to fly to the Moon and back more than 100,000 times, and a modified 747 has enjoyed the illustrious honor of serving as the *Air Force One* aircraft of choice for more than two decades and as a carrier for NASA's space shuttle fleet.

The embodiment of the term *jumbo jet,* later models of the Boeing 747 were capable of carrying up to 550 people on a given flight.

LOCKHEED 10/12 ELECTRA

In the early 1930s, Lockheed saw the need for a modern twin-engine transport that could keep pace with Boeing's Model 247 and Douglas's DC-2. Chief designer Hal Hibbard assigned some wind-tunnel tests to the University of Michigan, where a student named Clarence "Kelly" Johnson ended up running most of the tests on the Model 10 project. Lockheed hired Johnson as soon as he received his master's degree, and his first move was a bold one: He suggested adding a twin tail surface for mounting the rudders directly in the path of the engines' airflow, allowing greater control of the Electra. Not only did Lockheed accept his suggestion, but this multitail configuration became a company design hallmark. Johnson became a legend in aviation history for his experimental

work, and the first plane he helped design—that Model 10—was given the name Electra. It made its first flight in February 1934.

Around the time of its debut, a ruling by the U.S. Civil Aviation Authority banned all nighttime commercial passenger operations in single-engine aircraft. That made room in the market for the success of the Electra and its two twin-engine competitors, since airlines wanted an arsenal of planes that they could fly around the clock. Noncommercial operators also bought Electras—including Amelia Earhart, who was planning to pilot it in the around-the-world flight she would embark on in 1937. Sadly, that flight ended with her disappearance in the South Pacific.

The sleek and shiny Lockheed Electra was designed to compete for commercial airline orders with Boeing's Model 247 and Douglas's DC-2. It found its greatest fame, however, in private operations.

BELL X-1

The Bell X-1 holds a place in aviation history as the first airplane to fly faster than the speed of sound in controlled, level flight. The X-1 was also the first airplane in the X series of supersecret U.S. military experimental aircraft intended to test cutting-edge technologies. It was designed to imitate the aerodynamics of a Browning .50-caliber bullet, which was known to be stable in supersonic flight—and the X-1 looked the part. For its test flight, the rocket-engine plane was painted bright orange for visibility, carried aloft in the modified bomb bay of a Boeing B-29 Superfortress, and released.

Bell had big expectations for the X-1: The company was hoping to set records with its four-chamber engine built by Reaction Motors. The engine burned ethyl alcohol diluted with water, plus a liquid oxygen oxidizer. As dramatized in the film *The Right Stuff*, Bell test pilot Chalmers "Slick" Goodlin demanded a U.S.$150,000 bonus should he break the sound barrier in the X-1—a dream that didn't come true for him. Dissatisfied with the slow pace of the test program, the army air forces took over.

Finally, on October 14, 1947, a month after the Air Force split off from the army as a separate service, Captain Charles "Chuck" Yeager took off in the rocket-powered X-1—with *Glamorous Glennis* painted on the nose, in honor of his wife—from Muroc Army Air Field, now known as Edwards Air Force Base, near Palmdale, California. That day, he exceeded the speed of sound, and he did it for his regular Air Force pay. The story was leaked to the press, and earned the X-1 program the 1947 Collier Trophy for achievement in aviation.

In addition to being the first aircraft to break the sound barrier, the Bell X-1 was a product of the early government-driven, top-secret aircraft research that would forever recast the relationship between the Pentagon and the military industrial complex. The classified flight was leaked in December 1947, but the Air Force didn't confirm it until March 1948.

AERONCA CHAMP

The Aeronca Champion (almost universally called the Champ) is seemingly doomed to always play second fiddle to its predecessor, the iconic Piper Cub. It's easy to understand how the Champ could be a historical afterthought: For instance, the Piper Cub and the Champ came primarily in yellow—the Cub with a black lightning-bolt stripe and the Champ with an orange swoosh on the fuselage. Both had the same mission as a light trainer plane and the same basic configuration. Both were high-wing taildraggers with minimal power and tandem seating. But the Champ had some distinct advantages over its more famous competitor.

For one thing, it had a wider cabin than the Cub, as well as better visibility from the front seat. It also boasted more user-friendly controls, and many of its proponents make the case that the Champ's engineering in general was superior to that of the Cub. Unlike the Cub, which pilots fly solo from the rear seat, pilots could fly the Champ solo from the front. The plane was modified and improved in the years after its introduction during World War II: Follow-on versions came with more power and landing gear under the nose, and there was even a twin-engine version of the Champ.

After Aeronca's assets were acquired by Bellanca Aircraft, a series of improved models were produced in an on-again, off-again mode under a number of corporate entities for decades to come. While the Champ never attained the kind of lasting prestige acquired by its Piper competitor, it nevertheless amassed its own group of devoted admirers and was produced in numbers surpassing 10,000. American Champion Aircraft purchased the design in 1989, and in 2007 they put this beloved plane back into production, this time with sport pilots in mind.

Often confused with the Piper Cub, Aeronca's Champ had a wider cabin and more easily operated controls, and it could be flown solo from the front seat, affording much improved visibility in comparison to the Cub.

BOMBARDIER GLOBAL EXPRESS

When the Canadian-built Bombardier Global Express—and its main competition, Gulfstream's GV—emerged in the 1990s, they represented a new category of ultra-long-range business jets capable of exceeding a previously unheard of 6,905-mile (11,112.5-km) range. The original Global Express used the same Rolls-Royce turbofan engines as the GV—but the Bombardier jet had been designed on a clean sheet of paper, while the Gulfstream was an updated refinement of existing models. The Global Express did, however, use the same fuselage cross-section as Bombardier's Regional Jet line, giving it a roomier cabin than its main rival, which used a lengthened version of the same cabin width as its Gulfstream predecessors.

The wing design of the Bombardier jet also marked a significant step up in technology, with its advanced aerodynamics and sharp 35-degree wing sweepback. The Global Express quickly built itself a following when it first hit the market in 1998, and the market battle with Gulfstream led to spirited industry competition among engineers, including the range wars in which competitors stretched their flight profiles with successive models—each able to fly just a bit farther than the last. Today, Bombardier has dropped "Express" from the name of the plane and expanded the line to include the variants Global 5000 and 6000. The Global 7000 and 8000 are under development.

Advanced aerodynamics, the latest in jet-engine technology, and space-age avionics and guidance systems enable Bombardier's Global Express to live up to its name as a long-range business transport.

BEECHCRAFT KING AIR

The Beechcraft King Air 90 was introduced in 1964, the same year the Beatles made their U.S. premiere on the *Ed Sullivan Show*. Today, it remains the gold standard for turboprop twin-engine aircraft. Many King Airs, especially 90s, are flown by their owners. Their large, comfortable cabins, ability to take off without much runway, and predictable handling characteristics have made them ideal for family transportation and small-business executive travel—and sometimes both at the same time.

Ten years after the King Air 90 took to the skies, Beechcraft introduced the King Air 200 series. Powered by Pratt & Whitney's reliable PT6A turboprops, the twin-engine airplane was designed to carry eight to nine passengers. It was known to have excellent carrying capacity, speed, and durability—even President Lyndon Johnson trusted a King Air as his transport during his administration. Yet another version is widely used as a commuter airliner. With its reputation as a rugged, versatile performer that's also straightforward and easy to fly—"honest," in pilot parlance—it is no wonder that the series is still alive after nearly five decades.

The King Air models currently in production by Beechcraft are the 250 and 350i, which feature the latest in PT6A turboprop engines and glass-panel avionics. These modern updates ensure that the King Air will fly confidently into the rest of the twenty-first century.

The Beechcraft King Air, in continuous production since 1964, has outsold all of its turboprop competitors combined.

PILATUS PC-12

There's nothing in the skies remotely like this big, Swiss, pressurized single-engine turboprop, an airplane that's as comfortable in Cannes as it is in the Canadian Rockies. It can don white gloves and carry a full complement of passengers in private jetlike comfort, then switch to work mode for missions requiring heavy hauling. It can even perform both roles at once, with the rear cabin designated as the cargo hold and the front half dedicated to more luxurious passenger conveniences.

Introduced into service in 1994, the PT6-powered PC-12 has been a solid seller for Pilatus, thanks to its remarkable versatility. Among its virtues are field-ready landing gear; a midsize, highly reconfigurable, jet-class cabin; a huge side-loading utility door; and short-field capabilities that were previously unimaginable in an aircraft of this class. Best of all, it boasts the economy of a single-engine aircraft with the payload of some turboprop twins.

The most recent iteration of the PC-12 can carry even more weight and comes with Honeywell Primus Apex flat-panel avionics featuring precise moving map displays, traffic alerts, terrain databases, satellite weather, and programmable flight plans. Plus, it has a high-end BMW-designed interior. Despite all this luxury, the PC-12 is still an airplane that yearns for adventure.

The Pilatus PC-12's features and versatility compared with its operating cost make it a winner. It has served in civilian and military functions for many countries.

CONSOLIDATED B-24 LIBERATOR

Designed by Consolidated Aircraft in the late 1930s to outperform the popular B-17, the B-24 Liberator could pack more payload, fly faster, and go farther than its Flying Fortress contemporary. The all-metal, four-engine bomber's unique roller shutter bomb-bay doors were designed for reduced drag during combat, and the plane came equipped with the first tricycle landing gear outfitted on such a heavy aircraft. Roomy and capable of carrying up to 16,000 pounds (7.25 mt) of munitions, the Liberator earned the nickname the "Flying Boxcar."

While the B-24 never attained the kind of fame known by the B-17, it should have. The Liberator participated in all combat theaters and was produced in greater numbers than any other American aircraft during World War II. More than 18,400 were built, about half by the Ford Motor Company. The hangars that housed the Ford B-24 assembly line still exist at Willow Run Airport in Detroit, Michigan. Thousands of aircraft workers, including women immortalized by the title "Rosie the Riveter," turned out B-24s at a rate that reached 650 per month at the peak in 1944.

The most infamous B-24 mission of the war was launched against nine Romanian oil fields at Ploiesti on August 1, 1943. Of 177 B-24s that took off from their base in Libya, 54 were lost along with 660 crew members. Five Medals of Honor were awarded as a result of the mission, and that day came to be known as "Black Sunday."

Not as sleek or aesthetically pleasing as its fellow heavy bomber the Boeing B-17, Consolidated's B-24 was faster and carried a heavier bomb load.

MARCH OF AVIATION

From the beginning, the human race has dreamed of flying. But simply unlocking the secret of flight was not enough. There has always been the drive to go higher, faster, and farther. Not content to merely invade the sanctity of the atmosphere, we quickly harnessed flying machines for exploration, commerce, and, of course, war. The march of progress has been relentless, and now, a little more than a century after the first powered flight, we're perched on the edge of achieving private space tourism.

1895

The World's First Gliders – Otto Lilienthal

Otto Lilienthal became known as the "father of flight" for his experimentation with manned gliders. Closely resembling today's hang gliders, Lilienthal's aircraft were made of wood and fabric. He launched them from hills—some manmade—outside Berlin. His work became well known, and photographs of him flying were published around the world. Lilienthal died from injuries suffered in the crash of one of his gliders, but his place in aviation history is immortal.

1918

Strife-Fueled Innovation – World War I

We tend to think of World War I airplanes as the early, rickety, stick-and-fabric kites from which pilots dueled each other with revolvers. But by the end of the war, both sides were fielding sleek, robust, steel-tube-frame aircraft capable of 200 miles per hour (322 km/h) or more. Multiengine bombers could carry tons of explosives, and engines were achieving 400 horsepower. Aerodynamics advanced from the boxkite biplanes (and triplanes) held together with wire to strutless, full-cantilever monoplanes, such as the elegant Fokker DVIII.

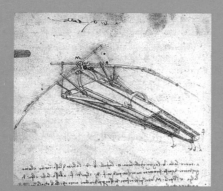

1505

First Plans for Flying Machines – Leonardo da Vinci

Renaissance man Leonardo da Vinci was fascinated by birds and flight. His drawings included a form of hang glider and a device resembling a helicopter. In 1505, he published his *Codex on the Flight of Birds,* a collection of eighteen folios that examined feathered flight and presented possible machines that could bring the gift of flight to man. Da Vinci experimented with stick-and-fabric versions of a number of potential flying machines, all without success. But the seed of innovation had been planted.

  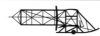

1783

Hot-Air Balloon – Montgolfier Brothers

In 1777, Joseph-Michel Montgolfier noticed that sheets hanging out to dry above a fire billowed up when filled with hot air. With his brother Étienne in September 1783, he launched a balloon attached to a basket holding a sheep, a duck, and a rooster. A month later, Étienne rose aloft in a larger balloon attached to an 80-foot (24.5-m) tether. In November, three men made the first free flight in a Montgolfier balloon, soaring 3,000 feet (914.5 m) above Paris and landing safely 14½ miles (23.5 km) away after a twenty-five minute flight.

1903

Wright Flyer – Wilbur and Orville Wright

A flurry of research on both sides of the Atlantic preceded the first officially recognized powered flight by the Wrights. In England, Sir George Cayley had identified the four forces of flight almost one-hundred years before Kitty Hawk; and in the United States, some claimed Gustave Whitehead achieved powered flight more than two years before December 17, 1903. But it was the two bicycle mechanics from Dayton, Ohio, who put all the pieces together—and patented the results.

1952

The New Jet Set – de Havilland

A scant five years after the first jet-powered military aircraft made their appearance, the airlines were knocking on the designers' doors for their own turbojet equipment. The de Havilland Comet was first to the party, but a series of puzzling fatal crashes doomed the type. Boeing's big gamble was the four-engine 707. By the early 1960s, it dominated the international airways, and the term "jet set" was coined to describe the world's elite travelers.

1939

Here Come the Jets – World War II

When the Germans invaded Poland in the fall of 1939, most of the world's air forces were fairly low-tech. The crucible of combat soon relegated the old-and-slow to the propwash of history, and ever faster, more powerful warbirds carved the skies at ever higher altitudes. In the end, even the propeller was rendered obsolete, as Axis and Allies developed the first jet fighters, causing jaw-dropping reactions from those unfortunates who chanced to fly in the path of progress.

1999

Personal Wingsuits – Birdman International

The first documented attempt at wingsuit-flying occurred in 1930, but in the late '90s, Croatian entrepreneurial daredevil Robert Pečnik designed a successful, safe wingsuit for skydivers and founded Birdman International with Finnish cohort Jari Kuosma. The suit features padded fabric between the arms and legs, providing lift much like the skin of a flying squirrel does. Ultimately, users land with the aid of a parachute, but not without first experiencing flight as nature intended for other species: just you, the open wind, and, of course, the sheer force of gravity.

1930

Piper Cub – William Piper and C. G. Taylor

The stock market crash of 1929 scuttled the dreams of millions of air-minded Americans. Flying was popular, especially after Lindbergh's heroic flight across the Atlantic, but it was expensive (sound familiar?). It took the engineering genius of C. G. Taylor and the business savvy of William T. Piper to bring to market a tiny, 40-horsepower airplane: the Cub.

1969

Supersonic Flight Goes Mainstream – Concorde

Military supersonic flight began in 1947 and Mach 2-plus became common. But the first civilian aircraft to dip a toe into supersonic operations was the Anglo-French Concorde. First flown in 1969, the Concorde program remains singular. There have been many attempts to launch follow-on supersonic aircraft—the in-development Aerion is a current example—but financial and environmental barriers (no one wants a sonic boom in their backyard) have scuttled all attempts—so far.

2013 and beyond

Private Space Tourism – Virgin Galactic

Nineteen-sixty-nine saw the first stroll on the moon by Neil Armstrong, an answer to President John Kennedy's challenge. While the ultimate in going "higher, faster, and farther" took place close to half a century ago, in the early decades of the new millennium, the buzz is all about private space travel. Richard Branson's Virgin Galactic space tourism company grew from the X-prize competition, and the company reports it has signed up more than 600 customers at around U.S.$250,000 per flight.

EMBRAER PHENOM 100

Brazilian manufacturer Embraer made its name in the mid-1990s for its regional airliners. It took the industry by storm with design and manufacturing know-how that no one expected. The company stepped into the private-jet market with corporate versions of its successful regional airliners, but it wasn't until it launched the Phenom 100 that it committed to developing a purpose-built bizjet.

Avoiding the industry-wide very-light-jet craze that never really found a mass market, Embraer focused on a jet that could serve owner-pilots, charter services, and small corporate flight departments. The twinjet hits a sweet spot among private buyers and air-taxi firms seeking a lower-priced business jet. It has a practical cabin size, seating up to six passengers. And unlike a lot of small jets left on the drawing board, it has a reasonably fast top speed of 449 miles per hour (722.5 km/h) and a decent range of 1,767 miles (2,843.75 km).

Perhaps most important of all, the Phenom 100 (and its larger sibling, the Phenom 300) come from a company recognized for its airline-quality standards in design and fabrication. In addition to its remarkable entry-level performance, the Phenom 100 features large flat-panel avionics, computer-controlled turbofan engines, and operating economies that rival some turboprop twins.

The Embraer Phenom 100 is designed to be operated by one pilot, and its
cockpit boasts an unprecedented level of automation and simplification—
allowing that single pilot to focus on the more fundamental aspects of flying.

VOYAGER

For most of the twentieth century, an around-the-world flight on one tank of gas was unimaginable. But Dick Rutan and Jeana Yeager made it happen, flying the Voyager: an odd-looking, twin-boom, carbon-fiber airplane first sketched on a napkin by Dick's brother, engineering legend Burt Rutan. For its takeoff roll from Edwards Air Force Base in California on December 14, 1986, the Voyager carried 7,011½ pounds (3.25 mt) of fuel—and that was the first and only time it ever flew with all seventeen tanks topped off. Onlookers cringed as the weighed-down plane's drooping wingtips scraped the runway, ripping one off and sending sparks flying, before the Voyager finally became airborne. Despite a rocky takeoff, Rutan and Yeager completed their historic mission in a little more than nine days and landed the Voyager safely back at Edwards.

By all accounts, the plane was an innovation marvel: Its immense carbon, Kevlar, and fiberglass frame weighed in at a mere 939 pounds (426 kg) with empty fuel tanks, and it was equipped with front and rear propellers each powered by a separate engine. The pilots rested in a 7½-by-2-foot (228.5-by-61-cm) cabin, where they ate powdered shakes and used an oversized rubber band to exercise during their brief but remarkable flight. The two did experience trouble with the rear engine shortly before landing, but were able to use the front engine to complete the journey. In a quirk of global mission rules, Federal Air Regulations define a flight that departs and lands at the same airport as local. So by strict interpretation of the rules, the Voyager's nine-day circumnavigation of planet Earth was logged as a local flight.

The Rutans and Jeana Yeager conceived the Voyager and its round-the-world flight as "The Last First" in aviation. Here, it's shown on display at the annual fly-in convention of the Experimental Aircraft Association in Oshkosh, Wisconsin.

MCDONNELL DOUGLAS F-4 PHANTOM

Initially designed for the U.S. Navy in the late 1950s, the McDonnell Douglas F-4 emerged from development in a class all its own. With the ability to fly at greater than twice the speed of sound and reach altitudes approaching 100,000 feet (30,480 m), the F-4 swiftly shattered more than a dozen world records while making it look easy. The Phantom was flown by all of the U.S. combat services, including the Air Force and the Marines. It carried a crew of two: the pilot sat up front and the radar intercept officer (also known as the RIO) sat behind. In a play on the preponderance of military acronyms, the second crew member was often jokingly called the "GIB"—"Guy In Back."

The Phantom was proficient in many roles, including air-to-air dogfighting, ground attack, and carrier operations, and thus the twinjet played a pivotal role in the Vietnam War. Navy Lieutenant Randy Cunningham became the first ace of the war—an unofficial title for a combat pilot or weapons officer who destroys five or more enemy aircraft—scoring victories three, four, and five by taking on three MiG-17s on May 10, 1972, from an F-4 cockpit. Captain Steve Ritchie became the first Air Force ace in an F-4 when he shot down five MiG-21s—two of them within the span of one minute and twenty-nine seconds. The F-4 saw combat in Desert Storm as well, and it ultimately would be produced in numbers greater than 5,000.

Without a doubt one of the most versatile combat aircraft of all time, the supersonic McDonnell Douglas F-4 Phantom dropped bombs, fired air-to-ground missiles, performed aerial reconnaissance, and excelled as a dogfighting platform.

CESSNA 150/152

If the Piper Cub taught the Greatest Generation to fly, the Cessna 150 and 152 were close behind in their significance. More than 30,000 of these versatile starter planes were produced, landing them among the top five most-manufactured civilian aircraft.

It all got started when, in the mid-1950s, Cessna took a look at its postwar tail-wheel-equipped 140 two-seater and decided to swap around the landing gear. The result was the 150: an all-metal, nimble trainer that was easy to handle on the ground. No one knows how many student pilots in the early days walked away from flying when they couldn't readily master the delicate, difficult art of landing a 140 "taildragger," but with the arrival of the 150, that obstacle was removed.

The 150's modest power and adequate—if not roomy—cabin size (ever wonder why there are more short pilots than tall ones?), led it to assume the role of forgiving teacher for thousands of budding pilots in the 1960s and '70s. The high wing afforded good downward visibility, the better to see your house while out practicing air work.

The 150 also had one essential element of a good trainer: resilient landing gear. Originally designed by 1930s air race legend Steve Wittman, the steel main gear legs are simple and robust to absorb awkward student landings. When Cessna switched engines from a 100-horsepower Continental to a slightly more powerful Lycoming, the 150 became the 152.

In production from 1958 to 1985, the Cessna 150/152 line saw many upgrades and design modifications over the years. For example, this Cessna 150 features a wrap-around "Omnivision" rear window and a speedy-looking swept-back tail, both introduced on the 1964 model.

AÉROSPATIALE-BAC CONCORDE

The concept of an airliner that could top the speed of sound was envisioned not long after U.S. Air Force test pilot Chuck Yeager successfully broke the sound barrier in 1947. Engineers in Britain, France, Russia, and the United States all began drawing up plans for planes that they hoped would accomplish the feat in the late 1950s. But Russia's efforts at building a supersonic transport ended in a tragic crash, and in the United States, economics scuttled Boeing's attempt to market a Mach-busting passenger jet. Neither Britain nor France could afford to go it alone, but, by government treaty, they designed and manufactured one of the marvels of twentieth-century technology together: Concorde.

Entering service in 1976, Concorde was incredibly efficient. For those who had the privilege of flying on it, a New York–to-London or Washington-to-Paris journey took less than half the time it would aboard a conventional jet. That's because Concorde cruised at approximately Mach 2.02, an astonishing 2.02 times the speed of sound—roughly 1,300 miles per hour (2,092.25 km/h), depending on altitude and atmospheric conditions. The impeccable design—from the delta- (triangle-) shape wings that provided amazing lift to the four turbojet engines—is what made such efficiency and speed possible. In fact, Concorde had to be finished with distinctive reflective white paint to avoid overheating its aluminum alloy structure while it endured the air friction caused by supersonic speeds. Sadly, mostly due to the costliness of manufacturing and operating Concorde, only twenty were built.

Concorde's distinctive droop-nose design is a hallmark of supersonic aircraft. It allows pilots to lower the nose on takeoff and landing for improved runway visibility.

The Me 262 owes its power to its two impressive jet engines—the first ever operational jet engines—and its aerodynamic elegance to airframe designer Ludwig Bölkow.

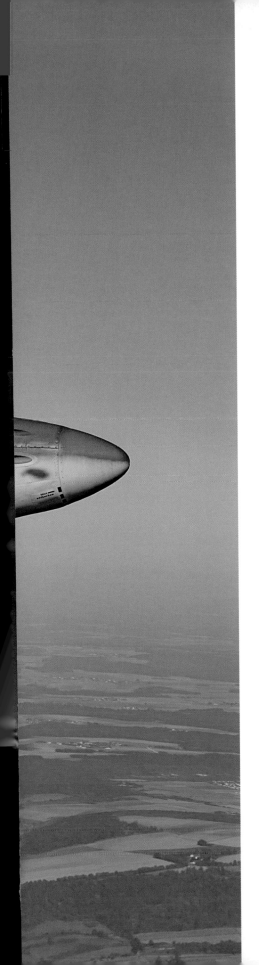

MESSERSCHMITT ME 262

"What the hell was that?" was the usual reaction from American fighter pilots who survived their first encounter with a Messerschmitt Me 262 "Schwalbe" ("swallow"). Barreling at more than 100 miles per hour (161 km/h) faster than the American P-51 Mustang, the 262—the first operational jet-powered fighter—could have been a game-changer in the air war over Europe. But Hitler insisted on using it as a ground-attack bomber instead. Faced with waves of Allied bombers every day, experienced Luftwaffe fighter aces, such as General Adolf Galland, pleaded for Me 262s to oppose the B-17s and B-24s and their escorting Mustang fighters in the air.

Despite his pleas, the Me 262 didn't see action as a fighter until 1944, and Galland's squadron of hand-selected pilots exacted a heavy toll in an ultimately losing cause. Jet-engine development had been progressing on both sides, with designers and engineers from both Germany and England at the vanguard of revolutionary technology. But Willy Messerschmitt's Me 262 had an edge, with swept wings that increased its performance at jet speeds. However, the Me 262's engines—jet-engine inventor Hans von Ohain's early Junkers Jumo 004s, each nearly the size of the Me 262's sleek, birdlike fuselage—were notoriously unreliable compared with jet engines today. With their high-fuel consumption, the twin-engine jets had little endurance, and American pilots learned to wait in ambush as they slowed to land at their airfields. Nonetheless, the Me 262's introduction marked an evolution away from piston-engine fighters.

The Sukhoi SU-27's ultra maneuverability makes it a captivating air-show favorite.

SUKHOI SU-27

The Soviet Union got wind of the U.S. Air Force's so-called "fourth Generation" design program—an initiative that ultimately led to the development of the McDonnell Douglas F-15—around 1969. Fearing that the Americans would leapfrog Soviet technology, the Soviet General Staff responded by designing its own advanced frontline fighter. Requirements included the following: a long range; good short-field takeoff and landing capability (even on unprepared surfaces); better than Mach 2 speed; the capability to carry heavy armament and other external equipment; and, perhaps most important, excellent agility in a dogfight. The Su-27 "Flanker" series was the result.

Since the Su-27 entered service in the early 1990s, improvements in engine performance, weaponry, and avionics have boosted its abilities—not just in the sky, but also in the quest for orders from foreign air forces, which is arguably a larger, more historically significant battlefield.

One giant leap for the Su-27 came when pilot Viktor Pugachev showed off the Cobra maneuver—in which the plane effectively stops its forward motion as it pulls vertical—for the first time in public at the 1989 Paris Air Show. With the Su-27's automated control system and ability to move slowly but stay aloft, Pugachev stunned viewers by briefly sustaining level flight at 120 degrees' angle of attack—a valuable capability in a dogfight.

SPECIFICATIONS

AERO COMMANDER

Manufacturer
Aero Design/North American Rockwell (USA)

Year introduced
1952 (original version with piston engines)

Number built
2,824 (all variants)

Wingspan 49 feet (15 m)

Length 36 feet, 10 inches (11.25 m)

Height 14 feet, 6 inches (4.5 m)

Useful load (includes fuel) 2,125 pounds (964 kg)

Maximum takeoff weight 6,750 pounds (3 mt)

Top speed 215 miles per hour (346 km/h)

Engines two Lycoming IO540s with 290 horsepower each

Number of seats six

Range 1,078 miles (1,735 km)

Facts of note
Beloved air-show performer Bob Hoover performed wildly famous aerobatic antics in his Aero Commander Shrike Commander, including pouring a glass of iced tea while executing a barrel roll.

The Aero Commander is probably the most changed design from how it started (a light piston twin) to how it ended up (a twin-engine jet). Along the way, its fuselage, wing, and tail surfaces were also modified.

AERONCA CHAMP

Manufacturer
Aeronautical Corp. of America (USA)

Year introduced
1945

Number built
10,000+

Wingspan 35 feet, 2 inches (10.75 m)

Length 21 feet, 6 inches (6.5 m)

Height 7 feet (2.25 m)

Useful load (includes fuel) 480 pounds (217.75)

Maximum takeoff weight 1,220 pounds (553.5 mt)

Top speed 100 miles per hour (161 km/h)

Engine Continental A-65 with 65 horsepower

Number of seats two

Range 460 miles (740.25 km)

Facts of note
The Champ was not introduced until the last year of World War II, but Aeronca's L-3 Defender—an early close relative of the Champ—saw service.

A civilian Aeronca 65TC, an ancestor of the Champ, was in the air over Hawaii when the Japanese attacked Pearl Harbor on December 7, 1941. It sustained battle damage from Japanese Navy Zero fighters, but landed safely with no injuries to the student or instructor. The airplane is on display at Hawaii's Gambo Flying Service.

AÉROSPATIALE-BAC CONCORDE

Manufacturer
British Aircraft Corp. Sud Aviation (England/France)

Year introduced 1976

Number built twenty

Wingspan 84 feet (25.5 m)

Length 204 feet (62.25 m)

Height 40 feet (12.25 m)

Payload 35,000 pounds (16 mt)

Maximum takeoff weight 412,000 pounds (16 mt)

Top speed Mach 2.02 (1,300 miles per hour [2,092 km/h])

Engines four Rolls-Royce/Snecma Olympus 593

Number of passenger seats 92–103

Range 4,500 miles (7,242 km)

Facts of note
Concorde weighed 173,500 pounds (78.75 mt) empty, yet it carried almost 211,000 pounds (95.75 mt) of fuel—36,500 pounds (16.25 mt) more than its own weight.

AH-64 APACHE

Manufacturer
Hughes/McDonnell Douglas/Boeing (USA)

Year introduced
1986

Number built
1,200+ (still in production)

Main rotor diameter 48 feet (14.75 m)

Length 58 feet, 2 inches (17.75 m)

Height 12 feet, 9 inches (4 m)

Useful load (includes fuel) 11,613 pounds (5.25 mt)

Maximum takeoff weight 23,000 pounds (10.5 mt)

Top speed 182 miles per hour (293 km/h)

Armament 30-mm gun; four hard points for rockets and/or Hellfire missiles

Engines two General Electric T700-series turboshafts with up to 2,000 shaft horsepower each

Number of seats two

Range 295 miles (474.75 km)

Facts of note
The Apache's first combat mission came in 1989 during the invasion of Panama, where it logged more than 240 combat hours of duty. General Carl Stiner, commander of Operation Just Cause, was impressed with the accuracy of the fire control system. He said, "You could fire that Hellfire missile through a window from 4 miles [6.4 km] away at night."

Through an accidental coincidence, the UHF radios used in early Apaches were the same as those used by the Air Force. That enabled interservice joint air attack teams (JAATs), and Apaches coordinated with Air Force A-10 Warthog attack jets and AV-8B Harrier II vertical-landing jets.

AIRBUS A380

Manufacturer
Airbus (France)

Year introduced
2007

Number built
101+ (still in production)

Wingspan 261 feet, 7 inches (79.75 m)

Length 238 feet, 7 inches (72.75 m)

Height 80 feet, 3 inches (24.5 m)

Useful load (includes fuel) 590,000 pounds (267.5 mt)

Maximum takeoff weight 1,200,000 pounds (544.25 mt)

Top speed Mach 0.89 (587 miles per hour [944.75 km/h])

Engines four Rolls-Royce Trent 970 series or Engine Alliance GP7270/7277 with 70,000-pound (31.75-mt) to 78,000-pound (35.5-mt) thrust each

Number of passenger seats up to 853; typically 525

Range 9,569 miles (15,399.75 km)

Facts of note
Outfitters of private jets have reported they are retrofitting A380s as high-end personal transports for certain high-net-worth individuals—very high net worth.

The A380 demonstrator made an appearance at the Experimental Aircraft Association fly-in in Oshkosh, Wisconsin. The brusque landing, conducted under a strong crosswind, raised eyebrows among some of the tens of thousands of pilots watching. One of the test pilots later shrugged off the criticism, saying it was normal for the conditions and perfectly safe.

ALBATROS D-SERIES

Manufacturer
Albatros Flugzeugwerke (Germany)

Year introduced
1916

Number built
approximately 2,500

Wingspan 29 feet, 8 inches (8.75 m)

Length 24 feet, 1 inch (7.25 m)

Height 8 feet, 10 inches (2.5 m)

Useful load (includes fuel) 551 pounds (250 kg)

Maximum takeoff weight 2,066 pounds (937 kg)

Top speed 116 miles per hour (186.75 km/h)

Armament two 7.92-mm machine guns firing through the propeller

Engine Mercedes liquid-cooled D.III with 150 horsepower

Number of seats one

Range approximately two hours' endurance

Facts of note
Two original Albatros fighters survived the war after being captured by Allied forces. One is on display at the National Air & Space Museum in Washington, D.C. The second is on display at the Australian War Memorial ANZAC Hall in Canberra, Australia.

Numerous Albatros replicas have been built, including one that is flown regularly at the Fantasy of Flight attraction in Polk City, Florida. It features an original Mercedes 200-horsepower inline engine and was built by the Vintage Aviator Ltd located in New Zealand.

ANTONOV AN-225 MRIYA

Manufacturer
Antonov (Russia)

Year introduced
1984

Number built
one (a second example is incomplete)

Wingspan 290 feet (88.5 m)

Length 275 feet, 7 inches (83.75 m)

Height 59 feet, 5 inches (18 m)

Useful load (includes fuel) 782,683 pounds (355 mt)

Maximum takeoff weight 1,411,000 pounds (640 mt)

Top speed 497 miles per hour (799.75 km/h)

Engines six SMKB Progress D-18 turbofans with 51,600-pound (23.5-mt) thrust each

Number of seats eight

Range 9,569 miles (15,399.75 km); 2,500 miles (4,023.25 km) when carrying maximum payload

Facts of note
The first commercial flight of the An-225 was on January 3, 2002, when it took off from Stuttgart, Germany, for Thumrait, Oman, in the Middle East. It carried 216,000 meals for American military personnel.

In April 2013, Russia announced plans to resume its space shuttle program, using the sole flying An-225 as an airborne launch vehicle.

AVIAT HUSKY

Manufacturer
Aviat Aircraft (USA)

Year introduced
1987

Number built
650+ (still in production)

Wingspan 35 feet, 6 inches (10.75 m)

Length 22 feet, 7 inches (6.75 m)

Useful load (includes fuel) 925 pounds (419.5 kg)

Maximum takeoff weight 2,250 pounds (1 mt)

Top speed 145 miles per hour (233.25 mph)

Engine Lycoming 0-360-A-1P with 180 horsepower

Number of seats two

Range 800 miles (1,287.5 km)

Facts of note
The Husky's center of gravity allows great leeway: There is flexibility where the bulk of the weight can go inside the cabin. Other airplanes may be able to carry as much weight as a Husky, but they require much more careful loading to maintain balance for safe flight.

The Aviat factory in Afton, Wyoming, used to belong to a company owned by Reuel Call, whose Call Aircraft Company produced a small low-wing cabin airplane known as the Call Air A-2. After World War II, the company made a go at building cropdusters, but the availability of surplus Stearman biplanes doomed that project, and the company failed. Frank Christensen moved in to the facility to build kits for his Christen Eagle biplane and Pitts Specials.

BAE HARRIER

Manufacturer
McDonnell Douglas (USA) /BAe (UK)

Year introduced
1969

Number built 143

Wingspan 30 feet, 4 inches (9.25 m)

Length 47 feet, 8 inches (14.25 m)

Height 11 feet, 8 inches (3.25 m)

Useful load (includes fuel and armaments) 17,000 pounds (7.75 mt)

Maximum takeoff weight 31,000 pounds (14 mt)

Cruise speed 662 miles per hour (1,065.5 km/h)

Armament two 25-mm cannons mounted on pods; eight hard points for pylon-mounted rockets, missiles, or bombs

Engine Pegasus 11 Mk 105

Number of seats one (two in trainer versions)

Combat range 345 miles (555.25 km)

Facts of note
In January 2007, British Harrier GR9 variants were sent to Kandahar, Afghanistan, to join NATO's International Security Assistance Force. After five years of continuous operation in the region, the last British Harriers were replaced by Tornado GR4s of the Royal Air Force. The Harriers flew a total of some 8,500 sorties and 22,000 hours in combat operations.

The last new-build Harrier rolled from the assembly line in 1997, but remanufactured airframes were completed up until 2003 when the BAe production line closed down for good.

BEDE BD-5

Manufacturer
Bede Aircraft (USA)

Year introduced
early 1970s

Number built
approximately 200 completed of 5,100 kits sold

Wingspan
14 feet, 6 inches (4.25 m)

Length 12 feet (3.75 m)

Height 5 feet, 2 inches (1.5 m)

Useful load (includes fuel) 732 pounds (332 kg)

Maximum takeoff weight 1,100 pounds (499 kg)

Top speed 200+ miles per hour (321.75+ km/h); 300+ miles per hour (482.75+ km/h) for jet version

Engine various, including Rotax, Subaru, and Honda

Number of seats one

Range 720 miles (1,158.75 km)

Facts of note
In the late 1960s, Jim Bede's original design, the BD-1 two-seater, was taken over by a Cleveland company, American Aviation. The young lawyer who ultimately ran the company and got the airplane certified was ex–Air Force pilot Russ Meyer, who later went on to head Cessna Aircraft and champion aviation tort reform.

Among BD-5 owner-pilots is Richard Bach, author of the 1970s bestseller *Jonathan Livingston Seagull.* He bought the tiny jet after his novel's success, and compared it favorably to the fighters he flew for the U.S. Air Force.

BEECHCRAFT BARON

Manufacturer
Beech Aircraft (USA)

Year introduced
1961

Number built
3,155 (all variants; the G58 is still in production)

Wingspan 37 feet, 10 inches (11.25 m)

Length 28 feet (8.5 m)

Height 9 feet, 7 inches (2.75 m)

Useful load (includes fuel) 1,944 pounds (881.75 kg)

Maximum takeoff weight 5,100 pounds (2.25 mt)

Top speed 236 miles per hour (379.75 km/h)

Engines two Continental IO-470-L with 260 horsepower

Number of seats four

Range 1,085 miles (1,746.25 km)

Facts of note

The last short-body Baron was the Model E55, built from 1970 until the final production year of 1982. In its twelve years of production, the price increased from just less than U.S.$84,000 to U.S.$219,500. A total of 433 were built.

Beech confused things with the names of its twin-engine light planes. The Twin Bonanza was nothing like a Bonanza. The Travel Air (a name resurrected from Walter Beech's early biplane days) was more like a twin-engine version of the Bonanza, but borrowed its slab-shaped tail surfaces from the T-34 Mentor military trainer. The name Baron spawned a succession of royalty-inspired names for later twins, including the Duke and the Duchess, and foreshadowing the Queen Air and King Air.

BEECHCRAFT BONANZA

Manufacturer
Beechcraft (USA)

Year introduced
1947

Number built
17,000+ (all variants)

Wingspan 32 feet, 9 inches (9.75 m)

Length 25 feet, 2 inches (7.5 m)

Height 6 feet, 6 inches (1.75 m), not including tail height

Useful load (includes fuel) 992 pounds (450 kg)

Maximum takeoff weight 2,550 pounds (1.25 mt)

Top speed 184 miles per hour (296 km/h)

Engine Continental E-185

Number of seats four

Range 1,100 miles (1770.25 km) with 20-gallon (75.75-L) auxiliary fuel tank

Facts of note

On February 3, 1959, singers Buddy Holly, Ritchie Valens, and J. P. "The Big Bopper" Richardson were killed along with pilot Roger Peterson when their chartered V-tail Bonanza crashed in Iowa, shortly after a late-night takeoff in bad weather. The incident inspired the 1971 song "American Pie" by Don McLean.

The unique V-tail configuration was the original Bonanza's signature design feature. Two rear control surfaces operate through a combiner that deflects them up and down in unison for pitch control (like an elevator), but deflects them differentially (one up and the other down) for yaw control, like a rudder. They are known as "ruddervators." Though it was thought the lower drag would increase speed, it turned out that later, otherwise comparable conventional-tail Bonanzas were just as fast.

Full disclosure: The author is the owner, pilot, and biggest fan of his own 1954 V-tail Bonanza.

BEECHCRAFT KING AIR

Manufacturer
Beechcraft (USA)

Year introduced
1964

Number built
3,550+

Wingspan 54 feet, 6 inches (16.5 m)

Length 43 feet, 9 inches (13 m)

Height 15 feet (4.5 m)

Useful load (includes fuel) 4,745 pounds (2.25 mt)

Maximum takeoff weight 12,500 pounds (5.75 mt)

Top speed 339 miles per hour (545.5 km/h)

Engine Pratt & Whitney Canada PT6A-42 with 850-shaft horsepower

Number of passenger seats up to thirteen

Range 2,075 miles (3,339.5 km)

Facts of note

Extending the regal model-name concept, the King Air is derived from the piston-engine Queen Air model, which has largely faded from view. The high-performance piston-powered Beech Duke, largely owner flown, is reputed as one of aviation's hot rods.

The King Air's tall landing gear—even with the smallest Model 90—gives it the aura of a much larger airplane. Combined with the associated folding airstair door, it's a design strategy that some credit with establishing the airplane's reputation as an imposing presence on the ramp.

BEECHCRAFT STAGGERWING

Manufacturer
Beechcraft (USA)

Year introduced 1933

Number built 785

Wingspan 32 feet (9.75 m)

Length 26 feet, 10 inches (8 m)

Height 8 feet (2.5 m)

Useful load (includes fuel) 710 pounds (322 kg)

Maximum takeoff weight 4,250 pounds (2 mt)

Top speed 212 miles per hour (341.25 km/h)

Engine Pratt & Whitney R985-AN-1 with 450 horsepower

Number of seats four

Range 670 miles (1,078.25 km)

Facts of note

Racers Louise Thaden and Blanche Noyes won the Bendix Trophy race in 1936 flying a D-17R Staggerwing; and Thaden won the Harmon Trophy for her effort. Jackie Cochran set a women's speed record in a Staggerwing at 204 miles per hour (328 km/h), also setting an altitude record at 30,000 feet (9,144 m).

BEECHCRAFT STARSHIP

Manufacturer
Beechcraft (USA)

Year introduced
1989

Number built
fifty-three

Wingspan 54 feet, 6 inches (16.5 m)

Length 46 feet (14 m)

Height 13 feet (4 m)

Useful load (includes fuel) 3,965 pounds (1.75 mt)

Maximum takeoff weight 14,900 pounds (6.75 mt)

Top speed 385 miles per hour (619.5 km/h)

Engines two Pratt & Whitney Canada PT6A-67A with 1,200-shaft horsepower each

Number of passenger seats six

Range 1,576 miles (2,536.25 km)

Facts of note

Burt Rutan's VariEze and LongEZ kitplanes were the harbinger of the Starship. They pioneered the composite construction and canard configuration that marked the Starship's legacy.

Burt Rutan's company, Scaled Composites, made the model for the Starship and became established as a developmental lab for radical new aeronautical concepts.

BELL X-1

Manufacturer
Bell Aircraft (USA)

Year introduced
1947

Number built one

Wingspan 28 feet (8.5 m)

Length 30 feet, 11 inches (9.25 m)

Height 10 feet (3 m)

Useful load (includes fuel) 5,250 pounds (2.5 mt)

Maximum takeoff weight 12,250 pounds (5.5 mt)

Top speed Mach 1.26 (959 miles per hour [1,543.25 km/h])

Engine Reaction Motors XLR-11-RM3 liquid fuel rocket with 6,000-pound (2.75-mt) thrust

Number of seats one

Range 5 minutes of endurance

Facts of note

The X-1 was painted International Orange for high visibility. It's the same color as the Golden Gate Bridge.

On January 5, 1949, Chuck Yeager took off from a runway in the X-1—the only time anyone ever did that—and reached an altitude of 23,000 feet (7 km) in 90 seconds.

BELL-BOEING V-22 OSPREY

Manufacturer
Bell-Boeing (USA)

Year introduced
1999

Number built
160 (408 on order)

Wingspan 45 feet, 10 inches (13.75 m)

Length 57 feet, 4 inches (17.25 m)

Height 22 feet, 1 inch (6.75 m)

Useful load (includes fuel) 14,369 pounds (6.5 mt)

Maximum takeoff weight 60,500 pounds (27.5 mt)

Top speed 316 miles per hour (508.5 km/h)

Armament one .50-caliber machine gun or one .30-caliber machine gun

Engines two Rolls-Royce Allison AE 1107C

Number of seats four crewmembers and thirty-two troops or 20,000 pounds (9 mt) of internal cargo

Range 1,011 miles (1,627 km)

Facts of note
Critics of the Osprey program are not without evidence. During the test phase from 1991 to 2000, there were four crashes resulting in thirty fatalities. Operational Ospreys have had three crashes with six deaths since it went into service in 2007.

The later safety record for the Osprey has been touted by the services as much improved. In February 2011, Marine Commandant General James Amos cited the tiltrotor as having half the mishap rate on flight hours of the average for the Marine fleet over the past ten years.

BENSEN B-8 GYROCOPTER

Manufacturer
Bensen Aircraft (USA)

Year introduced
1955

Number built
Unknown

Rotor diameter 20 feet (6 m)

Length 11 feet, 3 inches (3.25 m)

Height 6 feet, 3 inches (1.75 m)

Useful load (includes fuel) 253 pounds (114.75 kg)

Maximum takeoff weight 500 pounds (226.75 kg)

Top speed 55 miles per hour (88.5 km/h)

Engine McCulloch 4318AX with 72 horsepower

Number of seats one

Range 100 miles (161 km)

Facts of note
Spaniard Juan de la Cierva developed the first successful gyrocopter (he called it an "autogiro") in the early 1920s.

It took six tries, but the practical Cierva C.6 design incorporated hinges to permit the blades to flap at the mast.

Bensen submitted his B-8 Gyrocopter design to the U.S. Air Force for evaluation. It was designated the X-25, but no large contract resulted.

In the years before the first practical helicopters were developed, large passenger-carrying gyrocopters were envisioned that could serve remote locations where runways were not available.

BLÉRIOT XI

Manufacturer
Bleriot (France)

Year introduced
1909

Number built
unknown

Wingspan 25 feet, 7 inches (7.5 m)

Length 27 feet (8.25 m)

Height 8 feet, 10 inches (2.5 m)

Top speed 47 miles per hour (75.75 km/h)

Engine Anzani with 35 horsepower

Number of seats one

Range at least 26 miles (41.75 km)

Facts of note
Like Charles Lindbergh almost twenty years later, Louis Blériot was competing for a cash prize as the first to fly the English Channel. His competitors included Hubert Latham flying an Antoinette monoplane and Count de Lambert, who had purchased a pair of Wright biplanes from the American brothers. Blériot took a chance on the blustery weather and launched from near the French coast early on July 25, 1909. He beat his rivals to the punch and won the London Daily Mail's £1,000 prize.

Blériot's Channel-crossing airplane made a hard landing in England, damaging the landing gear and breaking the wooden propeller. The airplane never flew again, and today it hangs in the Musée des Arts et Metiers in Paris.

BOEING 314 CLIPPER

Manufacturer
Boeing (USA)

Year introduced
1938

Number built
twelve

Wingspan 152 feet (46.25 m)

Length 106 feet (32.25 m)

Height 20 feet, 5 inches (6 m)

Payload 10,000 pounds (4.5 mt)

Maximum takeoff weight 84,000 pounds (38 mt)

Top speed 210 miles per hour (338 km/h)

Engines four Wright R-2600-3 with 1,600 horsepower each

Number of seats ten crew; seventy-four passengers

Range 3,685 miles (5,930.5 km)

Facts of note
Pan Am christened its aircraft with geographic names such as Anzac Clipper, Dixie Clipper, and Pacific Clipper. The latter was en route from Hawaii to New Zealand when the Japanese attacked Pearl Harbor on December 7, 1941. It continued flying west around the world, landing at New York LaGuardia Airport almost a month later on January 6, 1942.

None of the twelve Boeing 314s survived beyond 1951. Most were scrapped; some were scuttled. In June 2012, a French recovery team located the Honolulu Clipper underwater, apparently lightly damaged, and recovery efforts are planned.

BOEING 737

Manufacturer
Boeing (USA)

Year introduced
1968

Number built
4,497 (all variants);
3,044 on order

Wingspan 117 feet, 5 inches, including winglets (35.75 m)

Length 138 feet (42 m)

Height 41 feet, 3 inches (12.5 m)

Useful load (includes fuel) 89,200 pounds (40.5 mt)

Maximum takeoff weight 187,700 pounds (85.25 mt)

Top speed Mach 0.82 (624¼ miles per hour [1,004.75 km/h]); cruises at March 0.78 (593¾ miles per hour [955.5 km/h])

Engines two CFM International CFM56-7 series

Number of passenger seats 108–215

Range 5,510 miles (8,867.5 km) fully loaded

Facts of note
At any given time, there are 1,250 Boeing 737s airborne throughout the world. Two 737s are taking off or landing every five seconds.

The Boeing Business Jet (BBJ)—the corporate-jet version of the transport—was envisioned in the early 1990s by then-GE president Jack Welch and Boeing CEO Philip Condit. They thought they might sell a few, but did not see it as a major program. To date, 138 of the 737-based BBJs have been delivered, with several more variants based on larger Boeing models, including the 787 Dreamliner.

BOEING 747

Manufacturer
Boeing (USA)

Year introduced
1970

Number built
1,458 (all variants)

Wingspan 224 feet, 7 inches (68.25 m)

Length 250 feet, 2 inches (76.25 m)

Height 63 feet, 6 inches (19.25 m)

Useful load (includes fuel) 502,100 pounds (227.75 mt)

Maximum takeoff weight 875,000 pounds (397 mt)

Top speed 614 miles per hour (988.25 km/h) with 555-mile-per-hour (893.25-km/h) cruise speed

Engines four Pratt & Whitney PW4062, General Electric CF6-80C2B5F, or Rolls-Royce RB211-524G/H

Number of seats 524 in a two-class configuration

Range 9,200 miles (14,806 km)

Facts of note
The Boeing 747 has served for decades as the United States' chief executive's transport—a.k.a. "Air Force One." Following the terror attacks of September 11, 2001, President George W. Bush took to the air and remained aloft until it was determined it was safe to land.

The truncated 747SP was developed in response to a request from Pan Am and Iran Air to produce an airliner capable of flying nonstop between New York and the Middle East. To enable that range, the SP variant was 48¼ feet (14.75 m) shorter than a standard 747 but with the same fuel load, enabling it to operate the longest nonstop route when launched.

BOEING B-17 FLYING FORTRESS

Manufacturer
Boeing Aircraft (USA)

Year introduced
1936

Number built 12,731 (by Boeing and under license by Douglas and Lockheed)

Wingspan 103 feet, 9 inches (31.5 m)

Length 74 feet, 4 inches (22.5 m)

Height 19 feet, 1 inch (5.75 m)

Payload up to 17,600 pounds (8 mt) of bombs on overloaded missions

Maximum takeoff weight 65,500 pounds (29.75 mt)

Top speed 287 miles per hour (462 km/h)

Armament between eleven and thirteen machine guns

Engines four Wright R-1820s (1,200 horsepower each)

Crew ten

Range 2,000 miles (3,218.75 km)

Facts of note

At first, the daylight bombing tactics proposed by the Americans were considered suicidal by the British. They had tried daylight bombing, but abandoned it for nighttime raids after German Luftwaffe fighters exacted too great a cost. Believing the Flying Fortress could defend itself, the Americans persisted, but it wasn't until the long-range P-51 Mustang fighter was able to protect B-17s all the way to the target and back that daylight bombing was shown to be an acceptable risk.

Best known for their service in Europe, B-17s were also a major weapon in the Pacific until the follow-on B-29 Superfortress appeared.

BOEING B-29 SUPERFORTRESS

Manufacturer
Boeing (USA)

Year introduced
1944

Number built 3,970

Wingspan 141 feet, 3 inches (43 m)

Length 99 feet (30.25 m)

Height 29 feet, 7 inches (8.75 m)

Useful load (includes fuel) 60,500 pounds (27.5 mt)

Maximum takeoff weight 135,000 pounds (61.25 mt)

Top speed 357 miles per hour (574.5 km/h)

Armament twelve .50 caliber machine guns; 20,000-pound (9-mt) bomb load

Engines four Wright R-3350-23 turbosupercharged radial engines with 2,200 horsepower each

Crew ten

Range 3,250 miles (5,230.25 km)

Facts of note

Fifi, the only remaining airworthy B-29, uses a hybrid form of the Wright R-3350 engine, modified to improve cooling. The original engines were problematic throughout the service life of the B-29.

The B-29's defensive machine gun turrets were aimed and fired remotely.

BOEING B-52 STRATOFORTRESS

Manufacturer
Boeing (USA)

Year introduced 1955

Number built 744

Wingspan 185 feet (56.5 m)

Length 159 feet, 4 inches (48.5 m)

Height 40 feet, 8 inches (12.25 m)

Useful load (includes fuel) 40 feet, 8 inches (137.5 mt)

Maximum takeoff weight 488,000 pounds (221.25 mt)

Top speed 650 miles per hour (1,046 km/h)

Armament 70,000 pounds (31.75 mt) of mixed ordnance, including bombs, mines, and missiles

Engines eight Pratt & Whitney TF33-P-3/103 turbofans with 17,000-pound (7.75-mt) thrust each

Crew five

Range 4,480 miles (7,209.75 km)

Facts of note

B-52s are planned for further upgrades through 2015, with service life projected to extend into the 2040s—and by then the plane will have enjoyed close to a century of operational flying.

The B-52's first actual combat mission (following years of use as a nuclear deterrent in the Cold War) was in June 1965 as part of Operation Rolling Thunder. Thirty B-52s attacked communist Viet Cong positions in South Vietnam.

BOEING-STEARMAN PT-17 BIPLANE

Manufacturer
Boeing Stearman (USA)

Year introduced
1934

Number built 10,000+

Wingspan 32 feet, 2 inches (9.75 m)

Length 24 feet, 9 inches (7.25 m)

Height 9 feet, 8 inches (2.75 m)

Useful load (including fuel and payload) 704 pounds (319.25 kg)

Maximum takeoff weight 2,635 pounds (1.25 mt)

Top speed 135 miles per hour (217.25 km/h)

Engine Continental 220-horsepower radial

Number of passengers two

Facts of note

More than once, instructors would forget to fasten their safety belts, as they were flying student after student every day. When they told their pupils to perform a loop, the instructor would fall out of the rear cockpit for an impromptu introduction to skydiving. The student's takeoff may have been under dual instruction, but the landing was solo.

The blueprints for the fabric cover on the wings of a Stearman included several small holes reinforced by grommets. In the event of a landing mishap that might have damaged the wing (known as a "groundloop"), the holes were for mechanics to reach inside and pluck the wing's internal truss wires. Hearing a wire with an "out of tune" note indicated there was internal damage to the wing that might not be visible from the outside.

BOMBARDIER GLOBAL EXPRESS

Manufacturer
Bombardier (Canada)

Year introduced
1998 (original model)

Number built
400+ (all variants; still in production)

Wingspan 94 feet (28.75 m)

Length 99 feet, 5 inches (30.25 m)

Height 24 feet, 10 inches (7.25 m)

Useful load (includes fuel) 49,750 pounds (22.5 mt)

Maximum takeoff weight 99,500 pounds (45.25 mt)

Top speed 590 miles per hour (949.5 km/h)

Engines two Rolls-Royce Deutschland BR710A2-20 turbofans with 14,750-pound (6.75-mt) thrust each

Number of passenger seats eight to nineteen

Range 7,080 miles (11,394.25 km)

Facts of note
When planning for the launch of the original Global Express in the early 1990s, Bombardier polled corporate pilots and flight departments on a number of design issues, including whether or not they would use computerized controls. The pilots vetoed the idea, and the Global Express flew with conventional cable-and-rod connections to its control surfaces.

Living up to its name, the Global Express has transcontinental range, being able to fly nonstop from Tokyo to New York. It can fly from any point on the globe to any other point with no more than one fuel stop.

CANADAIR CRJ

Manufacturer
Bombardier
(Canada)

Year introduced
1992

Number built
1,600+ (still in production)

Wingspan 69 feet, 7 inches (21 m)

Length 87 feet, 10 inches (26.5 m)

Height 20 feet, 5 inches (6 m)

Maximum takeoff weight 53,000 pounds (24 mt)

Engines two GE CF34-3A1 (CRJ100) CF34-3B1 (CRJ200) turbofans with 8,729 pounds (4 mt) of thrust

Number of passenger seats fifty

Range 2,307 miles (3,712.75 km)

Facts of note
The Canadair Regional Jet (CRJ) is based on the company's original Challenger business jet design. Canadair (since bought by Bombardier) bought the rights to complete the design and build that airplane from Bill Lear, the creator of the iconic first business jet that bore his name.

The CRJ family includes the CRJ100/200, each seating fifty passengers; the CRJ700 with seventy seats; the CRJ705 with seventy-five seats; the CRJ900 with ninety seats; and the CRJ1000 with one hundred seats.

CESSNA 150/152

Manufacturer
Cessna (USA)

Year introduced
1958 (original version)

Number built
23,949

Wingspan 33 feet, 4 inches (10 m)

Length 24 feet, 9 inches (7.25 m)

Height 8 feet, 6 inches (2.5 m)

Useful load (includes fuel) 490 pounds (222.25 kg)

Maximum takeoff weight 1,600 pounds (725.75 kg)

Top speed 123 miles per hour (198 km/h)

Engine Continental 0-200 with 100-horsepower (Lycoming 0-235 series in the later C-152 models)

Number of seats two

Range 421 miles (677.5 km)

Facts of note
Early Cessna 150s had a squared off, straight tail and razorback rear-cabin configuration with no rear window. These were later changed to a swept tail and wide "Omnivision" rear window.

Rolls-Royce powered Cessna 150s were also built under license in France. These production models used the same Continental 0-200 engine built under license by Rolls-Royce in England. They even had the iconic Rolls-Royce logo on the cylinder covers.

CESSNA 172 SKYHAWK

Manufacturer
Cessna Aircraft
(USA)

Year introduced
1956

Number built
43,000+

Wingspan 36 feet, 1 inch (11 m)

Length 27 feet, 2 inches (8.25 m)

Height 8 feet, 11 inches (2.5 m)

Useful load (includes fuel) 759 pounds (344.25 kg)

Maximum takeoff weight 2,450 pounds (1 mt)

Top speed 188 miles per hour (302.5 km/h)

Cruise speed 140 miles per hour (225.25 km/h)

Engine Lycoming IO-360 with 160 horsepower

Number of seats four

Range 801 miles (1,289 km)

Facts of note
In 1987, German teenage pilot Mathias Rust took off in a French-built Reims Cessna F172 from Helsinki-Malmi Airport and flew undetected through Russian airspace, landing in the middle of Red Square, Moscow.

On a fund-raising flight that spanned two calendar years, a new 1958 Cessna 172 set an endurance record, taking off from Las Vegas McCarran Airport on December 4, 1958, and remaining aloft for 64 days, 22 hours, 19 minutes, and five seconds, landing on February 4, 1959. Food and water were uploaded during the journey by rope from a speeding car, and fuel was transferred from the hose of a tanker truck, which matched speed with the airplane as it flew low over the runway.

Early Cessna 172s had square shaped tails, but in 1960, designers appealed to the look of modern jets by switching to a swept tail shape.

CESSNA 182 SKYLANE

Manufacturer
Cessna (USA)

Year introduced
1956

Number built
24,000+ (all variants)

Wingspan 36 feet (11 m)

Length 29 feet (8.75 m)

Height 9 feet, 4 inches (2.75 m)

Useful load (includes fuel) 1,140 pounds (517 kg)

Maximum takeoff weight 3,100 pounds (1.4 mt)

Top speed 173 miles per hour (278.5 km/h)

Engine Lycoming IO540-AB1A5 with 230 horsepower

Number of seats four

Range 1,070 miles (1,722 km)

Facts of note
Like the 172, the 182 is derived from its tailwheel-equipped ancestor. Cessna introduced its first tricycle-gear models in the mid-1950s. The 170 begat the 172; the 180, the 182.

From 1978 to the interruption in light aircraft production in 1986, Cessna offered a retractable-gear version of the Skylane, known as the 182RG. The narrow sprung-steel main gear legs folded backward and stowed in wells in the lower fuselage. Watching a Cessna retract its wheels after takeoff reminds one of a long-legged heron folding its legs against its body after taking wing.

CESSNA 195

Manufacturer
Cessna (USA)

Year introduced
1947

Number built 1,180

Wingspan 36 feet,
2 inches (11 m)

Length 27 feet, 4 inches (8.25)

Height 7 feet, 2 inches (2.25 m)

Useful load (includes fuel) 1,250 pounds (567 kg)

Maximum takeoff weight 3,350 pounds (1.5 mt)

Top speed 185 miles per hour (297.75 km/h)

Engine Jacobs R755 radial with 300 horsepower (240-horsepower Continental W670 in the Model 190)

Number of seats five

Range 800 miles (1,287.5 km)

Facts of note
The Cessna 195 spring steel landing gear was the result of Cessna purchasing the rights to air-race legend Steve Wittman's design. Throughout his life, Oshkosh, Wisconsin, native Wittman would smile every time he saw a Cessna land, knowing that its gear legs were supporting his aviation lifestyle.

The Cessna 190/195 line started at a price of U.S.$12,750 in 1947 and had nearly doubled to U.S.$24,700 by the time production ceased seven years later. In contrast, a Cessna 140 two-seater cost less than U.S.$3,500 ,and a 1954 Bonanza went out the door at U.S.$18,990.

CESSNA 208 CARAVAN

Manufacturer
Cessna (USA)

Year introduced
1984

Number built
2,000+ (still in production)

Wingspan 52 feet, 1 inch (15.75 m)

Length 47 feet, 7 inches (14.25 m)

Height 15 feet, 5 inches (4.5 m)

Useful load (includes fuel) 4,180 pounds (2 mt)

Maximum takeoff weight 8,750 pounds (4 mt)

Top speed 197 miles per hour (317 km/h)

Engine Pratt & Whitney PT6A-114A with 677-shaft horsepower

Number of passenger seats nine to fourteen

Range 1,240 miles (1,995.5 km)

Facts of note
Fourteen countries use the Caravan as a military platform, including the United States and Iraq.

The current Caravan features Garmin G1000 avionics, one of the most sophisticated flat-panel avionics suites available for general aviation aircraft, and a system included in all Cessna single pistons.

CESSNA 210/ P210

Manufacturer
Cessna (USA)

Year introduced
1957

Number built
9,240 (all variants)

Wingspan 36 feet, 9 inches (11 m)

Length 28 feet, 2 inches (8.5 m)

Height 9 feet, 8 inches (2.75 m)

Useful load (includes fuel) 1,697 pounds (769.75 kg)

Maximum takeoff weight 4,000 pounds (1.8 mt)

Top speed 235 miles per hour (378.25 km/h)

Engine Continental TSIO520R with 310 horsepower

Number of seats six

Range 1,036 miles (1,667.25 km)

Facts of note
Riley Conversions re-engined P210s with a 500-shaft-horsepower Pratt & Whitney Canada PT6A-12 turboprop engine. They were known as the Riley Turbine P210.

The pressure differential of the P210 was modest by today's standards at 3¼ pounds per square inch (1.5 kg per 2.5 cm²).

CESSNA CITATION I

Manufacturer
Cessna Aircraft (USA)

Year introduced
1971

Number built 689 (Citation I and I/SP)

Wingspan 47 feet, 1 inch (14.25 m)

Length 43 feet, 6 inches (13 m)

Height 14 feet, 3 inches (4.25 m)

Useful load (includes fuel) 5,219 pounds (2.25 mt)

Maximum takeoff weight 11,850 pounds (5.5 mt)

Top speed Mach .705 (536½ miles per hour [863 km/h])

Engines two Pratt & Whitney Canada JT15D-1B turbofans with 2,200-pound (998-kg) thrust each

Number of seats two pilots; five passengers

Range 1,528 miles (2,459 km)

Facts of note
The internal working name for the original Citation was FanJet 500, referring to the choice of the high-bypass fan engines, a relatively new technology at the time aimed at increasing efficiency. But the marketing department wanted a name with more pizzazz. At the time, Triple Crown-winner Citation had just died after a legendary horseracing career, so that's the name that was chosen.

On August 2, 1979, New York Yankees all-star catcher Thurman Munson died attempting to land his Citation I at Ohio's Akron-Canton Airport. The crash was largely attributed to his low number of hours logged as a pilot and his lack of experience with jet-aircraft operations.

CESSNA CITATION X

Manufacturer
Cessna (USA)

Year introduced
1996

Number built 330

Wingspan 63 feet, 7 inches (19.25 m)

Length 72 feet, 4 inches (22 m)

Height 19 feet, 2 inches (5.75 m)

Useful load (includes fuel) 14,100 pounds (6.5 mt)

Maximum takeoff weight 35,700 pounds (16.25 mt)

Top speed Mach 0.92 (700¼ miles per hour [1,127 km/h])

Engines two Rolls-Royce/Allison AE3007C/C1/C2 turbofans

Number of passenger seats twelve

Range 3,700 miles (5,954.5 km)

Facts of note
From its conception, it's always been a bit confusing as to whether the name of this jet was pronounced "ex," or represented the Roman numeral for "ten." The answer is: the latter.

The Citation X is the first of its family to have powered controls, a mix of electronically and hydraulically boosted surfaces. One of the design challenges was finding room in the wing for the hydraulic lines.

CESSNA CITATIONJET

Manufacturer
Cessna (USA)

Year introduced
1991

Number built
400 (all variants)

Wingspan 46 feet, 11 inches (14 m)

Length 42 feet, 7 inches (12.75 m)

Height 13 feet, 9 inches (4 m)

Useful load (includes fuel) 3,835 pounds (1.75 mt)

Maximum takeoff weight 10,700 pounds (4.75 mt)

Top speed 420 miles per hour (676 km/h)

Engines two Williams International FJ44-1AP with 1,965-pound (891.25-kg) thrust each

Number of seats four to ten

Range 1,495 miles (2,406 km)

Facts of note
The CitationJet was developed in parallel with a candidate for the U.S. Air Force and Navy Joint Primary Aircraft Training System (JPATS) contract. The trainer would have been a tandem two-seat aircraft with ejection seats, but it would have shared many systems with the Civilian CitationJet. Beechcraft won the contract with its Texan II single-turboprop trainer.

When Cessna introduced the CitationJet, it also developed a comprehensive training program designed to ensure owner-pilots would be well qualified to fly their airplanes, and that insurance companies' policies would encourage them to receive regular recurrent training. The result has been a remarkably safe history for a complex jet designed to be flown by non-professionals.

CIRRUS SR22

Manufacturer
Cirrus (USA)

Year introduced
2001

Number built
5,000+

Wingspan 38 feet, 4 inches (11.5 m)

Length 26 feet (8 m)

Height 8 feet, 11 inches (2.5 m)

Useful load (includes fuel) 1,375 pounds (623.75 kg)

Maximum takeoff weight 3,600 pounds (1.6 mt)

Top speed 213 miles per hour (342.75 km/h)

Engine Continental IO-550-N with 310 horsepower

Number of seats four to five

Range 1,207 miles (1,942.5 km)

Facts of note
When Cirrus first announced it would incorporate a whole-airplane parachute, many were skeptical. They argued that it would be safer to dedicate the added weight to more fuel capacity, since many accidents resulted from fuel starvation. We were wrong. To date, there have been thirty-three documented saves sparing the lives of sixty-nine Cirrus occupants.

The first Cirrus models incorporated conventional mechanical instruments, but those soon gave way to large computer-like screens. Flight and navigation information was displayed in high-resolution, jet-like format. Now, most new light airplanes feature "glass cockpits" as well.

CONSOLIDATED B-24 LIBERATOR

Manufacturer
Consolidated (USA)

Year introduced
1941

Number built
18,482

Wingspan 110 feet (33.5 m)

Length 67 feet, 8 inches (20.5 m)

Height 18 feet (5.5 m)

Useful load (includes fuel) 18,500 pounds (8.5 mt)

Maximum takeoff weight 65,000 pounds (29.5 mt)

Top speed 290 miles per hour (466.75 km/h)

Armament ten .50 caliber machine guns; up to 8,000 pounds (3.5 mt) of bombs

Engines four Pratt & Whitney R-1830 radial engines with 1,200 horsepower each

Crew eleven

Range 2,100 miles (3,379.5 km)

Facts of note
Navy pilot Joseph P. Kennedy, Jr., the older brother of President John Kennedy, was killed in an experimental adaptation of the Navy's version of the B-24. It was designed as a flying bomb. The crew would take off, set course, and then bail out, leaving the bomber to be flown by remote control from a shadow plane, then crashed into its target. Kennedy's plane mysteriously exploded prematurely before the crew had jumped.

For the B-24 assembly line at Willow Run, near Detroit, Ford recruited a team of ten little people from circus sideshows and the entertainment industry to buck rivets from inside tight spots, such as wingtips.

CURTISS JN-4 JENNY

Manufacturer
Curtiss (USA)

Year introduced
1915

Number built 6,813

Wingspan 43 feet, 8 inches (13 m)

Length 27 feet, 4 inches (8.25 m)

Height 9 feet, 11 inches (2.75 m)

Useful load (includes fuel) 530 pounds (240.5 kg)

Maximum takeoff weight 1,920 pounds (871 kg)

Top speed 75 miles per hour (120.75 km/h) with 60-mile-per-hour (96.5-km/h) cruise speed

Engine Curtiss OX-5 with 90 horsepower

Number of seats two

Endurance two hours

Facts of note
The Jenny is famous as the subject of one of the most valuable stamps ever. In 1918, a faulty press run printed the first sheet of 100 U.S.$0.24 air-mail stamps with an image of the Jenny upside down. In 2007, one of the stamps sold for just under U.S.$1 million.

A USMC JN-4 is credited with conducting the first dive-bombing attack in 1919 during the U.S. occupation of Haiti. With Marines trapped by Haitian Cacos rebels, pilot Lieutenant Lawson Sanderson loaded a bomb in a canvas mail bag attached to the Jenny's belly and improvised a bomb sight. He attacked the rebels, successfully diving to treetop height, nearly destroying the Jenny when he pulled out.

CURTISS MODEL D

Manufacturer
Curtiss (USA)

Year introduced
1909

Number built
unknown

Wingspan 38 feet, 3 inches (11.5 m)

Length 29 feet, 3 inches (8.75 m)

Height 7 feet, 10 inches (2 m)

Useful load (includes fuel) 600 pounds (272.25 kg)

Maximum takeoff weight 1,300 pounds (589.75 kg)

Top speed 50 miles per hour (80.5 km/h)

Engine Curtiss E-4 with 40 horsepower

Number of seats two

Endurance two-and-a-half hours

Facts of note
The Curtiss Pusher (Model D) was originally designed with a forward elevator control supplementing the rear-mounted elevator. On a demonstration flight, company pilot Lincoln Beachey ran into a fence while landing and damaged the forward elevator. He simply ripped off the forward control surfaces and flew his next demo flight without them. To his surprise, the airplane performed better. Subsequent models without the forward surfaces, referred to as the "Headless" Model D. Beachey, went on to become one of the most revered of Curtiss flyers, often chasing auto-racing legend Barney Oldfield around a fairground's oval tracks, the landing gear of his Pusher inches from Oldfield's head.

The Glenn H. Curtiss Museum in his hometown of Hammondsport, New York, on Lake Keuka, recreated and flew a 1911 Triad seaplane version of the Curtiss Pusher. The pilot reported that the non-standard controls were his biggest challenge. The ailerons are actuated by a shoulder yoke, the rudder by the control wheel (which functions like a ship's rudder), and the throttle by a foot pedal. Only the pitch control (pushing and pulling on the wheel) is conventional.

DASSAULT FALCON 7X

Manufacturer
Dassault Aviation (France)

Year introduced
2007

Number built 150+ (still in production)

Wingspan 86 feet (26.25 m)

Length 76 feet, 1 inch (23.25 m)

Height 25 feet, 8 inches (7.5 m)

Useful load (includes fuel) 34,928 pounds (15.75 mt)

Maximum takeoff weight 70,000 pounds (31.75 mt)

Top speed 593 miles per hour (954.25 km/h)

Engines three Pratt & Whitney Canada PW307A turbofans with 6,400 pounds (3 mt) of thrust each

Number of passenger seats up to fourteen

Range 6,836 miles (11,001.5 km)

Facts of note
The signature tri-jet configuration first found on the Falcon 50 offers unique advantages in performance and efficiency. For example, certification requirements for takeoff specify the need to display performance in the event of an engine failure. The Falcon 7X has 66 percent of its power available, while a twin-engine jet has only 50 percent.

The success of the Falcon line in the United States is attributed in part to its selection by Pan Am as the aircraft of choice for a new business jet division launched in the 1960s. The consultant sent to France to evaluate the Falcon was none other than Charles Lindbergh. Upon evaluating the Falcon 20, he wired back the message, "We have found our airplane."

DE HAVILLAND DHC-2 BEAVER

Manufacturer
de Havilland (Canada)

Year introduced
1947

Number built 1,657

Wingspan 48 feet (14.75 m)

Length 30 feet, 3 inches (9.25 m)

Height 9 feet (2.75 m)

Useful load (includes fuel) 2,100 pounds (952.5 kg)

Maximum takeoff weight 5,100 pounds (2,313.25 kg)

Top speed 158 miles per hour (254.25 km/h)

Engine Pratt & Whitney R-985 radial with 450 horsepower

Number of seats eight

Range 455 miles (732.25 km)

Facts of note
When de Havilland designers protested in 1946 that the features bush pilots wanted in the new Beaver would affect its cruise-speed numbers, the pilots responded, "You only have to be faster than a dog sled."

The doors of the Beaver allow the loading of a 45-gallon (170.25-L) fuel tank. And the reason there are two cargo doors is to permit loading with equal ease, whichever side of the dock the airplane taxied up to.

DIAMOND DA40

Manufacturer
Diamond Aircraft (Austria)

Year introduced
1997

Wingspan 39 feet, 2 inches (12 m)

Length 26 feet, 5 inches (8 m)

Height 6 feet, 6 inches (1.75 m)

Useful load (includes fuel) 890 pounds (403.75 kg)

Maximum takeoff weight 2,645 pounds (1.25 mt)

Cruise speed 175 miles per hour (281.75 km/h)

Engine Lycoming IO-360M1A with 180 horsepower

Number of seats four

Range 828 miles (1,332.5 km)

Facts of note
The DA40 first flew with a 100-hp Rotax 214 engine and is an expanded version of the two-seat DA20, which was marketed as an efficient trainer.

The DA40's overall accident rate is about one-eighth that of the rest of the general aviation fleet. Its sterling safety record is attributed in part to its high-aspect-ratio wing, which is resistant to stalling and spinning.

DOUGLAS DC-3

Manufacturer
Douglas Aircraft (USA)

Year introduced
1936

Number built
16,079 (including license-built versions)

Wingspan 95 feet, 2 inches (29 m)

Length 64 feet, 8 inches (19.5 m)

Height 16 feet, 11 inches (4.75 m)

Useful load (includes fuel) 8,334 pounds (3.75 mt)

Maximum takeoff weight 25,199 pounds (11.5 mt)

Top speed 230 miles per hour (370.25 km/h)

Engines two Pratt & Whitney R-1830s with 1,200 horsepower each, or two Wright R-1820s with 1,100 horsepower each

Number of passenger seats twenty-one to thirty-two

Range 2,125 miles (3,419.75 km)

Facts of note
In early 1941, a Chinese National Aviation Corp. DC-3 airliner was attacked on the ground by Japanese Zero fighters and its right wing was demolished. No replacements were available, so an earlier DC-2 wing was attached instead. Even though the DC-2 wing was 5 feet (1.5 m) shorter, the American pilots continued on the scheduled flight between Hong Kong and Chungking. This plane became known as the DC-2½.

In a 1933 publicity stunt designed to illustrate its performance, a Douglas DC-1 took off from Santa Monica, California, using only one of its two engines. It beat a Ford Trimotor to Albuquerque, New Mexico.

ECLIPSE 500

Manufacturer
Eclipse Aviation, now Eclipse Aerospace (USA)

Year introduced
2006

Number built 260

Wingspan 37 feet, 3 inches (11.25 m)

Length 33 feet, 1 inch (10 m)

Height 11 feet (3.25 m)

Useful load (includes fuel) 2,400 pounds (1 mt)

Maximum takeoff weight 5,950 pounds (2.75 mt)

Top speed 425 miles per hour (684 km/h)

Engines two Pratt & Whitney Canada PW610F turbofans with 900-pound (408.25-kg) thrust each

Number of seats six

Range 1,295 miles (2,084 km)

Facts of note
Sikorsky Aircraft—yes, the helicopter company—is now closely associated with the Eclipse jet program as a minority equity investor. With its worldwide customer support network, Sikorsky's backing means a lot to the future success of Eclipse.

One of the hallmarks of Eclipse production was said to be friction stir welding, the technology used to manufacture lightweight aluminum windows. The process was said to be the key to low-cost, high-volume production of thousands of Eclipse jets annually.

EMBRAER PHENOM 100

Manufacturer
Embraer (Brazil)

Year introduced
2007

Number built 269
(still in production)

Wingspan 40 feet, 4 inches (12.25 m)

Length 42 feet, 1 inch (12.75 m)

Height 14 feet, 3 inches (4.25 m)

Useful load (includes fuel) 3,384 pounds (1.5 mt)

Maximum takeoff weight 10,472 pounds (4.75 mt)

Top speed 449 miles per hour (722.5 km/h)

Engines two Pratt & Whitney Canada PW617F-E with 1,695 pounds (768.75 kg) of thrust each

Number of seats six to eight

Range 1,767 miles (2,843.75 km)

Facts of note
Ironically, the engine chosen for the Phenom was developed by Pratt & Whitney Canada for the Eclipse very light jet after its planned Williams engines could not deliver enough power. The switch was made to P&WC, and the resulting development was adopted by Embraer for its light jet, which developed much more successfully than the Eclipse program.

As a single-pilot-capable jet, Phenoms are often operated by owner-pilots, who have formed their own user group (complete with annual conferences).

ERCOUPE

Manufacturer
Engineering Research Co. (USA)

Year introduced
1940

Number built
5,685

Wingspan 30 feet (9.25 m)

Length 20 feet, 9 inches (6 m)

Height 5 feet, 11 inches (1.5 m)

Useful load (includes fuel) 511 pounds (231.75 kg)

Maximum takeoff weight 1,260 pounds (571.5 kg)

Top speed 110 miles per hour (177 km/h)

Engine Continental C-75-12 with 75 horsepower

Number of seats two

Range 300 miles (482.75 km)

Facts of note
When first introduced in 1940 as the airplane anyone could fly, the Ercoupe was put on display at Macy's department store in New York City. History does not record how many were sold as a result of the exposure.

Like several early light planes, the original Ercoupe qualifies under current Light Sport Aircraft rules (maximum takeoff weight of 1,320 pounds [598.75 kg] or less), making it eligible for pilots to fly without an FAA medical certificate. This feature increases the value of Ercoupes by opening up the market to many more potential buyers.

EXTRA 300

Manufacturer
Extra Flugzeugbau (Germany)

Year introduced
1990

Wingspan 24 feet, 3 inches (7.25 m)

Length 22 feet, 10 inches (6.75 m)

Height 8 feet, 8 inches (2.5 m)

Maximum takeoff weight 2,095 pounds (950.25 kg)

Top speed 253 miles per hour (407.25 km/h)

Engine Lycoming AEIO-540-L1B5 with 300 horsepower

Number of seats one to two

G-Range 10 Gs with one passenger and 8 Gs with two passengers

Facts of note
There are nine variants of the Extra 300, based on engine power, wing design, and other factors.

The two-seat version was introduced before the single-seat model, which appeared in 1992 with larger ailerons for greater roll rate.

FOKKER DR.1 TRIPLANE

Manufacturer
Fokker Flugzeugwerke (Germany)

Year introduced
1917

Number built 320

Wingspan 23 feet, 7 inches (7 m)

Length 18 feet, 11 inches (5.5 m)

Height 9 feet, 8 inches (2.75 m)

Useful load (includes fuel) 397 pounds (180 kg)

Maximum takeoff weight 1,292 pounds (586 kg)

Top speed 115 miles per hour (185 km/h)

Armament two 7.92-mm Spandau machine guns

Engine Oberursel Ur.II 9-cylinder rotary with 110 horsepower

Number of seats one

Range 185 miles (297.75 km)

Facts of note
The Dr.1 had full-cantilever wings, meaning all the structural strength came from internal spars and ribs. The initial prototype had no struts, but the final design included one outboard strut on each side connecting all three wings. It is said that was to prevent flexing, but it has also been said that the strut was added simply to placate skeptical pilots who did not trust the strength of the cantilever wing.

On the Fokker Triplane's Uberursel rotary engine (as well as the nearly identical French LeRhone from which it was copied), the crankshaft was fixed, and the nine cylinders rotated around it along with the massive wood propeller. This generated tremendous gyroscopic torque, making the fighter extremely unstable to fly compared with fighters with inline engines. Many replica Triplanes use small radial engines (in which the cylinders remain fixed and the crankshaft turns), which look similar to a rotary when at rest, but different when running.

FORD TRI-MOTOR

Manufacturer
Ford (USA)

Year introduced
1925

Number built 199

Wingspan 77 feet, 10 inches (23.5 m)

Length 50 feet, 3 inches (15.25 m)

Height 12 feet, 8 inches (3.75 m)

Useful load (includes fuel) 5,660 pounds (2.5 mt)

Maximum takeoff weight 13,500 pounds (6 mt)

Top speed 150 miles per hour (241.5 km/h)

Engines three Pratt & Whitney Wasp C radials with 420 horsepower each

Number of seats ten

Range 550 miles (885.25 km)

Facts of note
Among the Tri-Motor's direct competitors was the wooden Fokker trimotor, built at Teterboro, New Jersey. A Fokker crashed, killing famed Notre Dame football coach Knute Rockne, leading many to mistrust any non-metal airplane for airline use.

During the Battle of Bataan in the South Pacific in World War II, a Ford Tri-Motor was used to evacuate wounded and refugees from the oncoming Japanese forces. It would carry twenty-four passengers—more than twice its normal load—500 miles (804.75 km) on two flights a day. It was ultimately strafed and destroyed by the Japanese.

GENERAL ATOMICS PREDATOR DRONE

Manufacturer
General Atomics (USA)

Year introduced
1995

Number built 360

Wingspan 55 feet, 3 inches (16.75 m)

Length 27 feet (8.25 m)

Height 7 feet (2.25 m)

Useful load (includes fuel) 1,120 pounds (508 kg)

Maximum takeoff weight 2,250 pounds (1 mt)

Top speed 135 miles per hour (217.25 km/h)

Armament two hard points; Hellfire, Stinger, or Griffin air-to-surface missiles

Engine Rotax 214 with 115 horsepower

Number of seats zero

Range 776 miles (1,248.75 km)

Facts of note
Predator Drones were initially designed in the early 1990s to carry only high-definition cameras for reconnaissance, but when it was found they could also carry missiles, a new role was born.

In December 2002, a Predator engaged an Iraqi MiG-25, firing a stinger air-to-air missile at the manned fighter. The missile missed, and the MiG shot the drone down. This engagement is the first combat between a manned and remotely piloted unmanned aircraft.

GOSSAMER ALBATROSS

Manufacturer
AeroVironment/Paul MacCready and his team (USA)

Year introduced
1979

Number built two

Wingspan 100 feet (30.5 m)

Length 34 feet (10.25 m)

Height 16 feet (4.75 m)

Useful load 150 pounds (68 kg)

Maximum takeoff weight 220 pounds (99.75 kg)

Top speed 18 miles per hour (29 km/h)

Engines none (pusher propeller is powered by the pilot's pedaling)

Number of seats one

Range 35 miles (56.25 km)

Facts of note
On the Albatross's record-breaking Channel crossing, cyclist-pilot Bryan Allen gave up battling turbulence and headwinds and called for a tow. As he climbed to 15 feet (4.5 m) above the waves so the support team could attach the tow line, the turbulence subsided. He changed his mind and successfully landed in France.

Two Albatrosses were built, and Albatross I, which made the successful flight across the Channel, is on display at the Smithsonian Air & Space Museum at Dulles Airport outside Washington, D.C. The backup Albatross II was constructed in case the first Albatross were lost or damaged, and participated in the test program. It is on display in the Museum of Flight in Seattle, Washington.

GRANVILLE BROTHERS GEE BEE R SERIES

Manufacturer
Granville Brothers Aircraft (USA)

Year introduced
1932

Number built two

Wingspan 25 feet (7.5 m)

Length 17 feet, 8 inches (5.25 m)

Height 8 feet, 2 inches (2.5 m)

Useful load (includes fuel) 1,235 pounds (560.25 kg)

Maximum takeoff weight 3,075 pounds (1.4 mt)

Top speed 296 miles per hour (476.25 km/h)

Engine Pratt & Whitney R1340 with 800 horsepower

Number of seats one

Range 925 miles (1,488.75 km)

Facts of note
Steve Wolf and Delmar Benjamin built a flying replica of the Gee Bee R-2 in 1991, and Benjamin flew it at numerous air shows. He was adept at illustrating the "knife-edge" flying capability of the design. That airplane is currently on display at the Fantasy of Flight attraction in Polk City, Florida.

The speed records held by Gee Bees were specified as landplane records, because the Schneider Cup races of the same era involved seaplanes, and their speeds were significantly higher. For example, in 1931, the pontoon-equipped Supermarine S6.B (ancestor to the World War II Spitfire fighter) set a record of 407½ miles per hour (655.75 km/h).

GULFSTREAM G650

Manufacturer
Gulfstream (USA)

Year introduced
2012

Number built eight

Wingspan 99 feet, 7 inches (30.25 m)

Length 99 feet, 9 inches (30.5 m)

Height 25 feet, 4 inches (7.5 m)

Maximum takeoff weight 99,600 pounds (45.25 mt)

Top speed Mach 0.925 (704 miles per hour [1,133 km/h])

Engines two Rolls-Royce Deutschland BR725 turbofans with 6,100 pounds (2.75 mt) of thrust each

Number of passenger seats eleven to eighteen (two crew)

Range 8,050 miles (12,955.25 km)

Facts of note
The Gulfstream 650 was first estimated to have a top cruising speed of Mach 0.925 (704 miles per hour [1,133 km/h]), barely exceeding that of the Cessna Citation X. The Mach-0.92 (700¼-mile-per-hour [1,127-km/h]) Citation had reigned as the world's fastest business jet (and the fastest civil aircraft since the retirement of the supersonic Concorde airliner). Cessna reclaimed the title by adding more powerful engines and winglets on the Citation X, increasing its top speed to Mach 0.935 (711¾ miles per hour [1,145.5 km/h]).

The sweep angle of the G650 wing is 36 degrees, far exceeding the 27-degree sweep of the previous Gulfstream jet models.

HAWKER SEA FURY

Manufacturer
Hawker (UK)

Year introduced
1945

Number built 864

Wingspan 38 feet, 5 inches (11.5 m)

Length 34 feet, 8 inches (10.25 m)

Height 16 feet, 1 inch (4.75 m)

Useful load 3,260 pounds (1.5 mt)

Maximum takeoff weight 12,500 pounds (5.75 mt)

Top speed 460 miles per hour (740.25 km/h); a modified racer was unofficially recorded traveling at 547 miles per hour (880.25 km/h)

Armament four 20-mm Hispano cannons; and externally mounted rockets and bombs

Engine Bristol Centaurus XVIIC twin-row radial

Number of seats one

Range 700 miles (1,126.5 km); 1,040 miles (1,673.75 km) with drop tanks

Facts of note
On August 9, 1952, Royal Navy Sea Fury pilot Peter "Hoagy" Charmichael destroyed a Russian-built MiG-15 jet fighter in air-to-air combat. His Sea Fury survives to this day in civil registry, and flies in its original Royal Navy markings from its owner's home base in Australia.

One reason the Royal Navy continued development of the Sea Fury after the land-based Fury was discontinued

Armament two 7.92-mm MG-15 machine guns; one 13-mm MG-131 machine gun (dorsal position) and 1,100 pounds (499 kgs) of bombs

Engines three BMW 132 with 715 horsepower

Number of seats seventeen passengers (airline configuration); eighteen troops (military configuration)

Range 540 miles (869 km)

Facts of note
Martin Caidin restored the oldest existing Ju-52, which he dubbed *Iron Annie*. He chronicled the restoration in his book *The Saga of Iron Annie*. In 1984, he sold his plane to Lufthansa, which renamed it *Tempelhof* and still uses it as a VIP transport.

Ju-52s were used by the thinly disguised German Luftwaffe during the Spanish Civil War. The engagement was used as a try-out for several German aircraft, including the Messerschmitt Me-109 fighter.

is that the Seafires in service at the time (carrier-based versions of the Supermarine Spitfire) were not optimized for flying from a ship. Their poor forward visibility and narrow-track landing gear made them difficult to control on deck.

Angola, when it was attacked by a MiG-23. One air-to-air missile hit the left engine, causing it to fall from the business jet. The fire from the falling engine attracted the MiG's second heat-seeking missile, and the pilots were able to land the jet safely on an emergency airfield.

Seventeen separate countries have operated the Hawker line as military aircraft. They include the United States as well as the United Kingdom.

Germany's technological advancement, as well. A few months later, American Olympian Jesse Owens disappointed the Fuhrer by dominating the summer Olympic games in the German capital of Berlin by winning four gold medals.

On its ill-fated journey, the *Hindenburg* carried only half its full complement of passengers: thirty-six. There were nearly double the number of crewmembers on board—sixty-one in total—including twenty-one trainees. This was the first of ten scheduled round trips for 1937, and the return trip to Europe was fully booked. Many were planning to attend the coronation of King George VI and Queen Elizabeth in London the following week.

HAWKER
SIDDELY HS-125

Manufacturer
Hawker Beechcraft (UK/USA)

Year introduced
1962

Number built
650 (800s only)

Wingspan 54 feet, 4 inches (16.5 m)

Length 51 feet, 2 inches (15.5 m)

Height 18 feet, 1 inch (5.5 m)

Useful load (includes fuel) 12,330 pounds (5.5 mt)

Maximum takeoff weight 28,000 pounds (12.75 mt)

Top speed 514 miles per hour (827.25 mph)

Engines two Honeywell TFE731-BR turbofans with 4,660 pounds (2 mt) of thrust each

Number of passenger seats eight to thirteen

Range 3,040 miles (4,892.5 km)

Facts of note
Hawkers are tough: On August 7, 1988, a BAe-125 operated by the government of Botswana was carrying the country's president to a meeting in nearby Luanda,

HINDENBURG

Manufacturer
Luftschiffbau Zeppelin (Germany)

Year introduced
1936

Number built one

Diameter 135 feet (41.25 m)

Length 803 feet, 10 inches (244.75 m)

Engines four Daimler Benz 16-cylinder DB 602 diesels

Passenger capacity seventy-two passenger sleeping berths, plus forty crew members and twelve stewards

Range transatlantic

Facts of note
On June 23, 1936, the *Hindenburg*'s passenger manifest included celebrated boxer Max Schmeling, returning home to Germany to meet with Adolf Hitler after defeating American Joe Louis at New York's Yankee Stadium. Seen as proof of the superiority of the German Aryan race, Schmeling's victory over the Brown Bomber was heavily exploited by Nazi propaganda. The flight home on the airship was a way of highlighting

JUNKERS JU-52

Manufacturer
Junkers (Germany)

Year introduced
1932

Number built
4,845

Wingspan 95 feet, 10 inches (29 m)

Length 62 feet (19 m)

Height 14 feet, 10 inches (4.25 m)

Useful load (includes fuel) 5,945 pounds (2.75 mt)

Maximum takeoff weight 20,270 pounds (9.25 mt)

Cruise speed 165 miles per hour (265.5 km/h)

KITFOX

Manufacturer
Kitfox Aircraft, originally Denney Aerocraft (USA)

Year introduced
1984

Number built
unknown (close to 5,000 kits produced)

Wingspan 32 feet (9.75 m)

Length 18 feet, 5 inches (5.5 m)

Height 5 feet, 8 inches (1.5 m)

Useful load (includes fuel) 550 pounds (249.5 kg)

Maximum takeoff weight 1,200 pounds (544.25 kg)

Top speed 125 miles per hour (201.25 km/h)

Engine Rotax 912 with 80 horsepower

Number of seats two

Range 785 miles (1,263.25 km)

Facts of note
In all, there were four Kitfox models developed by Denney Aerocraft. The final iteration, known as the Kitfox 4-1200 (also known as the Classic 4) came out in 1991 with beefed-up structure for a maximum gross weight of 1,200 pounds (544.25 kg) and expanded tail surfaces for improved control.

In 1992, Denney sold the rights to the Kitfox design to SkyStar Aircraft, which began design of a new Kitfox Series 5, a larger version with more useful load and a bigger cabin. The company also introduced the ultralight version, the Kitfox Lite, with only one seat. A company called Belite Aircraft, based in Wichita, Kansas, still produces a Kitfox Lite ultralight derivative. It has a single seat and carbon-fiber wings, spars, ribs, and struts, lowering its empty weight to 245 pounds (111.25 kg).

LEARJET 23

Manufacturer
Learjet (USA)

Year introduced
1964

Number built 104

Wingspan 35 feet,
7 inches (10.75 m)

Length 43 feet, 3 inches (13 m)

Height 12 feet, 7 inches (3.75 m)

Useful load (includes fuel) 6,350 pounds (3 mt)

Maximum takeoff weight 12,499 pounds (5.75 mt)

Top speed 561 miles per hour (902.75 km/h)

Engines two General Electric CJ610-4 turbojets with 2,850 pounds (1.25 mt) of thrust each

Number of passenger seats six

Range 1,830 miles (2,945 km)

Facts of note
Bill Lear's almost equally famous wife, Moya, was the daughter of vaudeville legend Ole Olsen, whose show "Hellzapoppin" reigns as the longest running production in Broadway history. Lear was notorious for his philandering, and was rumored to have once locked himself with a paramour in the cabin of a Learjet while it was flying on autopilot. According to the legend, he had to break down the cockpit door with an axe to get back in and land before running out of fuel.

With its large wingtip fuel tanks, a Learjet 23 flying overhead was often mistaken for a military jet with missiles attached.

LOCKHEED
10/12 ELECTRA

Manufacturer
Lockheed (USA)

Year introduced
1935

Number built 149

Wingspan 55 feet
(16.75 m)

Length 38 feet, 7 inches (11.5 m)

Height 10 feet, 1 inch (3 m)

Useful load (includes fuel) 4,006 pounds (1.75 mt)

Maximum takeoff weight 10,500 pounds (4.75 mt)

Top speed 202 miles per hour (325 km/h)

Engines two Pratt & Whitney R.985 Wasp Junior SB radials with 450 horsepower

Number of passenger seats ten

Range 713 miles (1,147.5 km)

Facts of note
The airplane shown in the final scene of the 1942 film *Casablanca* is a Lockheed Electra Model 12. In parts of the final scene, the airplane that characters Victor and

Ilsa are about to board is visible in the background. Because of new wartime restrictions on location shots at airports, those segments were shot on a sound stage, and the airplane in the background is a smaller-scale wood replica. The studio introduced fog to disguise the ruse, and the ground crew seen moving about were portrayed by little people, so the small size of the phony airplane would not be apparent.

It's perhaps symbolic that Dick Merrill's May 1937 round-trip crossing of the Atlantic Ocean in a Lockheed Electra was carrying newsreel footage of the crash of the *Hindenburg* airship on its eastbound leg as well as photographs of King George VI's coronation on the return trip. Many passengers booked to return to Europe on the *Hindenburg* were invitees to the coronation ceremony. Merrill received the Harmon Trophy for his two-way crossing flight. The same airplane was later used for routine transportation for Bata Shoes executives throughout Europe.

LOCKHEED
C-130
HERCULES

Manufacturer
Lockheed Martin
(USA)

Year introduced
1954 (first variant)

Number built more than 2,300 (all models; C-130J currently in production)

Wingspan 132 feet, 7 inches (40.25 m)

Length 97 feet, 9 inches (29.5 m)

Height 38 feet, 3 inches (11.5 m)

Useful load (includes fuel) 72,000 pounds (32.75 mt) with 45,000-pound (20.5-mt) payload

Maximum takeoff weight 155,000 pounds (70.25 mt)

Top speed 366 miles per hour (589 km/h)

Engines four Allison T56-A-15 turboprops with 4,590-shaft horsepower each

Number of seats five crew, ninety-two passengers, seventy-two combat troops, or sixty-four paratroops

Range 2,050 miles (3,299.25 km)

Facts of note
In 1963, U.S. Navy Lieutenant James Flatley III performed twenty-nine touch-and-go landings aboard the USS *Forrestal*, setting a record for the largest and heaviest aircraft to land on an aircraft carrier. In tests to determine the practicality of using C-130s on carriers, Flatley also performed twenty-one takeoffs and full-stop landings on the deck, without benefit of catapults or arresting cables. In the end, carrier operations were deemed too risky, and Flatley was awarded the Distinguished Flying Cross for his courage.

The Blue Angels may be a Navy jet team, but it's supported by U.S. Marines operating a special C-130 named *Fat Albert*. The transport travels with the jet team and sometimes shares the limelight, performing fly-bys for the crowd. Until 2009, Fat Albert would demonstrate rocket-assisted takeoffs (RATO), an exciting display

of smoke and fire. RATO has long been an obsolete technology, except for show. The practice was terminated when the Marines ran out of rockets.

LOCKHEED
CONSTELLATION

Manufacturer
Lockheed (USA)

Year introduced
1945

Number built 856

Wingspan 126 feet, 2 inches (38.5 m)

Length 116 feet, 2 inches (35.25 m)

Height 234 feet, 9 inches (71.25 m)

Useful load (includes fuel) 65,300 pounds (29.5 mt)

Maximum takeoff weight 137,500 pounds (62.25 mt)

Top speed 377 miles per hour (606.75 km/h)

Engines four Wright R3350 radial turbo compound supercharged with 3,250 horsepower

Number of seats sixty-two to ninety-five

Range 5,400 miles (8,690.5 km)

Facts of note
The first Constellation delivered to Air France in June 1946 was bought for U.S.$45,000 in 1976 and flown into tiny Greenwood Lake Airport in New Jersey. The landing must have been quite a sight. Greenwood Lake's 3,471-foot (1-km) runway is only 60 feet (18.25 m) wide, less than half the Connie's wingspan. The owner used the grounded airliner's cabin area for a lounge. After the airport was sold to the state, it was later converted to be the flight school's office building.

LOCKHEED
MARTIN
F-22 RAPTOR

Manufacturer
Lockheed Martin
(USA)

Year introduced
2005

Number built 187

Wingspan 44½ feet (13.5 m)

Length 62 feet (19 m)

Height 16¾ feet (5 m)

Useful load 28,330 pounds (12.75 mt)

Maximum takeoff weight 60,000 pounds (27.25 mt)

Cruise speed Mach 1.8 (1,370 miles per hour [2,204.75 km/h])

Armament two AIM Sidewinders; six AIM AMRAAMs; one M61A2 20mm Gatling gun; two 1,000-pound (453.5-kg) JDAMs; eight 250-pound (113.5-kg) SDBs; four external hard points for weapons or external fuel tanks

Engines two Pratt & Whitney F119-PW-100 with 35,000-pound (15.75-mt) thrust

Number of seats one

Range Pilot-limited, with aerial refueling

Facts of note
A ban on exports of the F-22 made continuation of the program a significant challenge for Lockheed Martin. The good news for the company was the preference for the cheaper F-35 in the international community, also a LockMart product.

Dispatch reliability isn't a strong suit for the Raptor, with a mission-ready rate of only 62 percent in 2004, though it improved to 70 percent in 2009 and was expected to achieve 85 percent once it reached 100,000 flight hours.

LOCKHEED
P-38
LIGHTNING

Manufacturer
Lockheed (USA)

Year introduced
1939

Number built
9,923

Wingspan 52 feet
(15.75 m)

Length 37 feet, 10 inches (11.25 m)

Height 12 feet, 10 inches (3.75 m)

Useful load (fuel and payload) 10,460 pounds (4.75 mt)

Maximum takeoff weight 21,600 pounds (9.75 mt)

Top speed 443 miles per hour (713 km/h)

Armament one 20-mm cannon; four .50 caliber Browning machine guns; 2,000 pounds (907.25 mt) of bombs or rockets

Engines two Allison V-1710-27/29

Number of seats one

Range 2,600 miles (4,184.25 km)

Facts of note
Charles Lindbergh flew combat missions in P-38s in the South Pacific as a factory representative, and is said to have shot down Japanese aircraft.

The P-38 is the only U.S. fighter to see continued production from the beginning to the end of World War II.

LOCKHEED
SR-71
BLACKBIRD

Manufacturer
Lockheed Aircraft
(USA)

Year introduced
1964

Number built thirty-two

Wingspan 55 feet, 7 inches (16.75 m)

Length 107 feet, 5 inches (32.5 m)

Height 18 feet, 6 inches (5.5 m)

Payload 3,500 pounds (1.5 mt)

Maximum takeoff weight 172,000 pounds (78 mt)

Cruise speed 2,000 miles per hour (3,218.75 km/h)

Engines two Pratt & Whitney J58-P4s with 34,000 pounds (15.5 mt) of thrust each

Number of seats two

Range 3,337 miles (5,370.5 km)

Facts of note
Even flying in rarified air at 80,000 feet (24,384 m), the SR71 needed air conditioning to sustain life for the crew, since air friction heated the surface to 500 degrees Fahrenheit (200° C).

The same pressure suits used for the Blackbird, made by David Clark Co. of Worcester, Massachusetts, were also used for crews of NASA's space shuttles.

LUSCOMBE MODEL 8 SILVAIRE

Manufacturer Luscombe (USA)

Year introduced 1937

Number built 5,867 (all variants)

Wingspan 35 feet (10.75 m)

Length 20 feet (6 m)

Height 6 feet, 3 inches (1.75 m)

Useful load (includes fuel) 530 pounds (240.5 kg)

Maximum takeoff weight 1,400 pounds (635 kg)

Top speed 128 miles per hour (206 km/h)

Engine Continental C90 with 90 horsepower

Number of seats two

Range 500 miles (804.75 km)

Facts of note
Donald Luscombe served as an ambulance driver in France during World War I. It was there that he received his first airplane ride. Upon returning to Davenport, Iowa, he bought a surplus Curtiss Jenny and learned to fly.

Lusocmbe's first involvement in the aviation industry was with an Iowa company called Central States Aero Co., which hired a young farmhand named Clayton Folkerts to design an airplane that became known as the Monocoupe. Despite his lack of engineering training, Folkerts went on to a storied air racing career, designing and building his own mounts. Luscombe branched out from the Monocoupe design to develop his own unique aircraft, culminating with the Model 8 Silvaire.

MCDONNELL DOUGLAS F-15 EAGLE

Manufacturer McDonnell Douglas (USA)

Year introduced 1976

Number built 1,198

Wingspan 42 feet, 10 inches (12.75 m)

Length 63 feet, 9 inches (19.25 m)

Height 18 feet, 6 inches (5.5 feet)

Useful load (includes fuel) 40,000 pounds (18.25 mt)

Maximum takeoff weight 68,000 pounds (30.75 mt)

Top speed Mach 2.5 (1,650 miles per hour [2,655.5 km/h])

Armament one 20-mm six-barrel Gatling cannon; eleven external hard points for auxiliary fuel tanks, bombs, and missiles (AIM-7 Sparrow, AIM-120 AMRAAM, or AIM-9 Sidewinder)

Engines two Pratt & Whitney F100-100/220 turbofans with 17,450 pounds (8 mt) of thrust each

Number of seats one to two

Range 1,222-mile (1,966.5-km) combat radius; 3,450-mile (5,552.25-km) ferry range with auxiliary fuel tanks

Facts of note
Besides the United States, the F-15 has served the air forces of Israel, Japan, and Saudi Arabia. More than half the 104 confirmed combat kills credited to F-15s have been with the Israeli Air Force. It has been in service in Israel since 1977.

There were thirty-nine confirmed air-to-air victories tallied by U.S. forces against Iraqi forces during the Gulf War. F-15s accounted for all but three. Thirty-four occurred during the 1991 operation. They included fights with five MiG-29s, two MiG-25s, eight MiG-23s, two MiG-21s, four Su-25s, four Su-22s, one Su-7, six Mirage F1s, one Il-76 cargo plane, one PC-9 trainer, and two Mi-8 helicopters. Most were destroyed by missiles.

MCDONNELL DOUGLAS F-4 PHANTOM

Manufacturer McDonnell Douglas (USA)

Year introduced 1960

Number built 5,195

Wingspan 38 feet, 5 inches (11.5 m)

Length 63 feet (19.25 m)

Height 16 feet, 6 inches (4.75 m)

Useful load (includes fuel) 31,567 pounds (14.25 mt)

Maximum takeoff weight 61,795 pounds (28 mt)

Top speed Mach 2.23 (1,697½ miles per hour [2,731.5 km/h])

Armament 18,650 pounds (8.5 mt) of bombs, rockets, and missiles

Engines two General Electric J79-GE-79A turbojets with 11,905 pounds (5.5 mt) of thrust each or 17,845-pound (8-mt) thrust with afterburner

Number of seats two

Range 422 miles (679.25 km)

Facts of note
Though it excelled as a fighter, the F-4 could also carry twice the bomb load that B-17s typically carried during World War II.

The Phantom is the only aircraft type to be flown by both the Air Force Thunderbirds jet demonstration team and the Navy Blue Angels.

F-4 Phantoms were used by eleven other nations besides the United States. Iran used its Phantoms in the Iran-Iraq war, and Israel had great success with the type in combat during several Arab-Israeli clashes.

MESSERSCHMITT BF-109

Manufacturer Messerschmitt (Germany)

Year introduced 1935

Number built 33,984 (all models, plus another 842 under license after the war)

Wingspan 32 feet, 6 inches (9.75 m)

Length 29 feet, 7 inches (8.75 m)

Height 8 feet, 2 inches (2.5 m)

Useful load (includes fuel) 1,047 pounds (475 kg)

Maximum takeoff weight 7,495 pounds (3.5 mt)

Top speed 398 miles per hour (640.5 km/h)

Armament two 13-mm machine guns; one 20-mm cannon

Engine Daimler Benz DB 605A-1 inverted V-12 with 1,455 horsepower

Number of seats one

Range 621 miles (999.5 km) with exterior drop tank

Facts of note
The model designation of the Messerschmitt 109 remains controversial. The original company where Willy Messerschmitt worked was Bayerische Flugzeugwerke—so initially they were called Bf 109s. When the corporate structure changed, they were called Me 109s. Most Allied fighter pilots during the war used the latter, but some insist the "Bf" prefix is more correct.

During German bombing raids during the Battle of Britain, the escorting Bf 109's limited fuel supply gave it only ten minutes' combat time over London, a limitation the defending British used to their advantage when attacking the bombers. Many a German fighter pilot ran out of gas and ditched his 109 in the Channel or crash-landed short of his base in France.

MESSERSCHMITT ME 262

Manufacturer Messerschmitt (Germany)

Year introduced 1944

Number built 1,430

Wingspan 41 feet, 6 inches (12.5 m)

Length 34 feet, 9 inches (10.5 m)

Height 11 feet, 6 inches (3.5 m)

Useful load (includes fuel) 7,354 pounds (3.25 mt)

Maximum takeoff weight 15,720 pounds (7.25 mt)

Top speed Mach 0.84 (639½ miles per hour [1,029.25 km/h])

Armament four 30-mm cannons; twenty-four 55-mm rockets

Engines two Junkers Jumo 004B1 turbojets with 1,980 pounds (898 kg) of thrust each

Number of seats one

Range 652 miles (1,049.25 km)

Facts of note
After the death of Willy Messerschmitt, Me 262 pilot Hans Mutke reported exceeding the speed of sound in a 90-degree dive on April 9, 1945. There is no documentation, and skeptics say the aircraft behavior described by Mutke is consistent with very high but subsonic speeds.

Replica Me-262s are flying. With the cavernous nacelles required for the giant Jumo engines of the original, there is plenty of room for more reliable modern engines, such as the General Electric J85. The Me 262 Project, based in Everett, Washington, is producing a single-seater, a two-seat trainer model, and a pair of convertibles that are switchable between the two configurations. Other replicas have been built in Germany.

MIKOYAN-GUREVICH MIG-15

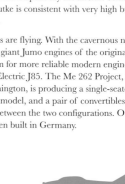

Manufacturer Mikoyan and Gurevich (Russia)

Year introduced 1949

Number built 12,000 plus another 6,000 under license

Wingspan 33 feet, 1 inch (10 m)

Length 33 feet, 2 inches (10 m)

Height 12 feet, 2 inches (3.75 m)

Useful load (includes fuel) 5,560 pounds (2.5 mt)

Maximum takeoff weight 13,460 pounds (6 mt)

Top speed 668 miles per hour (1,075 km/h)

Armament one 37-mm N-37 cannon; two 23-mm NR-23 cannons mounted in the nose

Engine Klimov RD-45 (Rolls-Royce Nene copy)

Number of seats one

Range 1,230 miles (1,979.5 km) with auxiliary external fuel tanks

Facts of note
Between December 1950 and June 1955, there were at least eleven incidents around the world involving MiG-15s exchanging fire with Allied aircraft.

American pilots were frustrated by the political borderline of the Yalu River, which runs between China and Korea. They could only watch as the MiGs climbed to safe altitudes, waiting to cross the river and attack the Allies until they had the advantage.

MITSUBISHI A6M ZERO

Manufacturer
Mitsubishi (Japan)

Year introduced
1940

Number built
10,939

Wingspan 39 feet, 4 inches (12 m)

Length 29 feet, 9 inches (8.75 m)

Height 10 feet (3 m)

Maximum takeoff weight 5,313 pounds (2.5 mt)

Top speed 331 miles per hour (532.75 km/h)

Armament two cowling-mounted 7.7-mm machine guns; two wing-mounted 20-mm cannons

Engine Nakajima Sakae radial with 950 horsepower

Number of seats one

Range 1,929 miles (3,104.5 km)

Facts of Note
The American code name was Zeke, the first of a series of male "hillbilly" code names for Japanese fighters that was to also include Rufe for the floatplane version of the Zero. Bombers got female names (Betty and Judy, for example).

In June 1942, a Zero crashed near Dutch Harbor, Alaska, after being damaged by ground fire. Its pilot was killed when it flipped over, but the Zero was discovered mostly intact, and shipped to Naval Air Station North Island in San Diego for evaluation. The opportunity to examine—and test-fly—a Zero was an invaluable boost to American pilots who had to fight against it.

MOONEY M20J

Manufacturer
Mooney Aircraft
(USA)

Year introduced
1977

Number built 377

Wingspan 36 feet, 1 inch (11 m)

Length 24 feet, 8 inches (7.25 m)

Height 8 feet, 4 inches (2.5 mt)

Useful load (includes fuel) 1,069 pounds (485 kg)

Maximum takeoff weight 2,740 pounds (1.25 mt)

Top speed 201 miles per hour (323.5 km/h)

Engine Lycoming IO-360 with 200 horsepower

Number of seats four

Range 794 miles (1,277.75 km)

Facts of note
Mooney's 201 led to the M20K model, which was turbocharged with a top speed of 252 miles per hour (405.5 km/h). Its name? The 252.

Mooneys were traditionally designed with their tail surfaces' trailing edges canted forward, rather than swept back. Though some claim it was an aerodynamic decision, it is generally believed that Al Mooney just liked the way it looked. Hecklers on the ramp will sometimes tell Mooney pilots that the tail was installed backward.

NORTH AMERICAN AT-6 TEXAN

Manufacturer
North American
Aviation (USA)

Year introduced
1935

Number built 15,495

Wingspan 42 feet (12.75 m)

Length 29 feet (8.75 m)

Height 11 feet, 8 inches (3.25 m)

Useful load (includes fuel) 1,459 pounds (661.75 kg)

Maximum takeoff weight 5,617 pounds (2.5 mt)

Top speed 208 miles per hour (334.75 kmh)

Armament three .30 caliber machine guns in the wings and nose for gunnery training

Engine Pratt & Whitney R-1340 with 600 horsepower

Number of seats two

Range 730 miles (1,174.75 km)

Facts of note
T-6s were modified to look like Japanese Zero fighters for the movie *Tora! Tora! Tora!* Some of those airplanes were used in other movies, including *Final Countdown* and also the television series *Black Sheep Squadron*.

Designed and manufactured by the same company as the P-51 Mustang fighter, the T-6 is still considered the best training ship for pilots transitioning to the Mustang.

NORTH AMERICAN F-86 SABRE

Manufacturer
North American
Aviation (USA)

Year introduced
1949

Number built 9,860

Wingspan 37 feet (11.25 m)

Length 37 feet, 1 inch (11.25 m)

Height 14 feet, 1 inch (4.25 m)

Useful load (includes fuel) 4,027 pounds (1.75 mt)

Maximum takeoff weight 15,198 pounds (7 mt)

Top speed 687 miles per hour (1,105.5 km/h)

Armament six .50 caliber machine guns mounted in the nose

Engine General Electric J47-GE-27 with 5,910 pounds (2.75 mt) of thrust

Number of seats one

Range 1,525 miles (2,454.25 km)

Facts of note
Sabres were built under license by Canadair in Canada. The last variant of these, the Sabre 6, is considered the best of the breed.

On May 18, 1953, Jacqueline Cochran became the first woman to break the sound barrier. She was flying a specially modified Canadair Sabre 3. Alongside Cochran was her pal, Chuck Yeager, who was the first to fly faster than the speed of sound in the Bell X-1 rocket plane five years earlier.

NORTH AMERICAN P-51 MUSTANG

Manufacturer
North American
Aviation (USA)

Year introduced
1941

Number built 16,766

Wingspan 37 feet (11.25)

Length 32 feet, 3 inches (9.75 m)

Height 13 feet, 5 inches (4 m)

Maximum takeoff weight 12,100 pounds (5.5 mt)

Top speed 437 miles per hour (703.25 km/h)

Engine Packard Merlin V-1650-7 (Rolls-Royce designed, V-12, liquid cooled)

Number of seats one

Range 1,650 miles (2,655.5 km) with external fuel tanks

Facts of note
The cooling configuration used on the Mustang, with its distinctive belly scoop for the radiator, was designed using data purchased from Curtiss Aircraft, the company that designed the P-40 that the Mustang replaced.

Top scoring Mustang ace Charles Preddy was killed on Christmas Day 1944 by friendly fire as he was pursuing a German fighter low to the ground in his P-51, dubbed *Cripes 'a Mighty III*.

NORTHROP GRUMMAN B-2 STEALTH BOMBER

Manufacturer
Northrop
Grumman (USA)

Year introduced
1997

Number built twenty-one

Wingspan 172 feet (52.5 m)

Length 69 feet (21 m)

Height 17 feet (5.25 m)

Useful load (includes fuel) 218,000 pounds (99 mt)

Maximum takeoff weight 376,000 pounds (170.5 mt)

Top speed Mach 0.92 (700 miles per hour [1,126.5 km/h])

Engines four General Electric F118-GE-100 with 17,300 pounds (7.75 mt) of thrust each

Crew two

Range 6,900 miles (11,104.5 km)

Facts of note
The B-2 achieves its stealth properties thanks to a shape that deflects radar signals, materials that absorb the radar pulses, and placement of the engines that shields their heat from detection by thermal devices.

The B-2 made its combat debut during the Kosovo War of 1999. Taking off from their bases in Missouri, B-2 flew all the way to Kosovo, delivered their ordnance, and flew all the way back, using aerial refueling. Their maintenance requirements are such that it makes more sense to keep them at their home base than to have the support team set up in the field.

PIAGGIO AERO P.180 AVANTI

Manufacturer
Piaggio (Italy)

Year introduced
1990

Number built 260
(still in production)

Wingspan 46 feet (14 m)

Length 47 feet, 4 inches (14.25 m)

Height 13 feet, 1 inch (4 m)

Useful load (includes fuel) 4,100 pounds (1.75 mt)

Maximum takeoff weight 11,550 pounds (5.25 mt)

Top speed 458 miles per hour (737 km/h)

Engines two rear-facing Pratt & Whitney Canada PT6A-66 turboprops with 850 horsepower each

Number of seats one to two crew; up to nine passengers

Range 1,737 miles (2,795.5 km)

Facts of note
The Avanti's forward wing is often mistakenly called a canard, but it does not have moving control surfaces.

The upgraded Avanti II was certified in 2005 and features updated engines for higher speed and improved fuel efficiency, plus advanced avionics.

PILATUS PC-12

Manufacturer
Pilatus (Switzerland)

Year introduced
1994

Number built
1,200+ (still in
production)

Wingspan 53 feet, 3 inches
(16.25 m)

Length 47 feet, 3 inches (14.25 m)

Height 14 feet (4.25 m)

Useful load (includes fuel) 4,583 pounds (2 mt)

Maximum takeoff weight 10,450 pounds (4.75 mt)

Top speed 313 miles per hour (503.75 km/h)

Engine Pratt & Whitney Canada PT6A-67 with 1,200-shaft horsepower

Number of passengers six to nine

Range 1,753 miles (2,821.25 km)

Facts of note
PlaneSense is a fractional ownership company operating PC-12s. Under the program, co-owners buy a share of an airplane and are eligible to fly on any one of the thirty-four aircraft in the combined fleet. PlaneSense is headquartered in New Hampshire and is the largest fractional operator of PC-12s in the world.

PIPER J-3 CUB

Manufacturer
Piper Aircraft (USA)

Year introduced
1938

Number built
19,073 (including
L-4 military variants)

Wingspan 35 feet, 3 inches (10.75 m)

Length 22 feet, 5 inches (6.75 m)

Height 6 feet, 8 inches (1.75 m)

Maximum takeoff weight 1,220 pounds (553.5 kg)

Cruise speed 75 miles per hour (120.75 km/h)

Engine Continental A-65-8 with 65 horsepower

Number of seats two

Range 220 miles (354 km)

Facts of note
Initially, W. T. Piper and C. G. Taylor were partners in producing the Taylor Chummy light airplane and designing the first Cub, the E-2. They later became rivals when Taylor branched off from Piper and designed the side-by-side Taylorcraft.

William Piper got into the airplane business when one of his partners in oil exploration invested in the Taylor brothers' aircraft manufacturing without his knowledge. Piper took to the business, however, and made his name synonymous with light aircraft.

PIPER PA-28 CHEROKEE

Manufacturer
Piper (USA)

Year introduced
1960

Number built
32,800+ (still in
production)

Wingspan 30 feet (9 m)

Length 23 feet, 4 inches (7 m)

Height 7 feet, 4 inches (2.25 m)

Useful load (includes fuel) 949 pounds (430.5 kg)

Maximum takeoff weight 2,150 pounds (975.25 kg)

Top speed 142 miles per hour (228.5 km/h)

Engine Lycoming O320 series with 150 horsepower

Number of seats four

Range 535 miles (861 km)

Another big user of PC-12s is the Royal Flying Doctor Service of Australia. Now with thirty-six PC-12s, the group was the launch customer for the PC-12 in 1994.

Facts of note
Widely available at rock-bottom prices, used Cherokees are popular among flight schools. They are rugged, easy to maintain, and forgiving of students' awkward beginner technique.

Piper Cherokees were not ideally suited to floatplane operations, but some were mounted on pontoons.

PIPER PA-32 CHEROKEE SIX

Manufacturer
Piper Aircraft (USA)

Year introduced
1965

Number built
close to 8,000
(includes all
variants)

Wingspan 33 feet (10 m)

Length 28 feet (8.5 m)

Height 8 feet (2.5 m)

Useful load (includes fuel) 1,612 pounds (731.25 kg)

Maximum takeoff weight 3,400 pounds (1.5 mt)

Top speed 174 miles per hour (280 km/h)

Engine Lycoming IO540-K1A5 with 300 horsepower

Number of seats six

Range 840 miles (1,351.75 km)

Facts of note
Cherokee Sixes are often used for patient transfer because of their wide cabin doors. They are popular among charity organizations that volunteer to fly patients for treatments when they cannot afford transport or when their condition does not allow airline travel.

With the wide range in age of Cherokee Sixes on the market, values vary widely as well. Early models with Hershey Bar wings can run less than half that of later Saratogas with tapered wings and modern avionics.

PIPER PA-46 MALIBU

Manufacturer
Piper Aircraft (USA)

Year introduced
1983

Number built
404 (Continental-
powered model only)

Wingspan 43 feet (13 m)

Length 28 feet, 5 inches (8.5 m)

Height 11 feet, 4 inches (3.25 m)

Useful load (includes fuel) 1,746 pounds
(792 kg)

Maximum takeoff weight 41,000 pounds (18.5 mt)

Top speed 269 miles per hour (433 km/h)

Engine Continental TSIO520BE with 310 horsepower

Number of seats six

Range 1,789 miles (2,879 km)

Facts of note
A company named JetPROP converts piston-powered Malibus to turboprops. Their conversion competes directly with Piper's own turboprop Meridian.

When Piper introduced the non-pressurized Malibu Matrix, it came with an Avidyne Entegra avionics suite, rather than the Garmin G1000 found in the Meridian and the Mirage.

PITTS SPECIAL

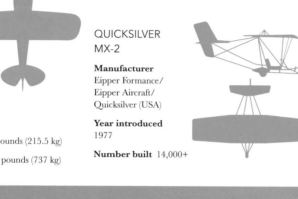

Manufacturer
Aviat Industries
(USA)

Year introduced
1944

Number built
unknown

Wingspan 20 feet (6 m)

Length 18 feet, 9 inches (5.5 m)

Height 6 feet, 7 inches (1.75 m)

Useful load (includes fuel) 475 pounds (215.5 kg)

Maximum takeoff weight 1,625 pounds (737 kg)

Top speed 210 miles per hour (338 km/h)

Engine Lycoming with 200 horsepower (S1); Lycoming with 260 horsepower (S2)

Number of seats one (S1); two (S2)

Range 319 miles (513.5 km)

Facts of note
EAA past president Tom Poberezny, Charlie Hillard, and Gene Soucy formed an aerobatic demonstration team called the Red Devils, flying Pitts S1s. They later switched to Christen Eagles and changed their name to the Eagles.

At the time of his death in 2005 at eighty-nine, Curtis Pitts was working on the design of his Pitts Model 14, a fire-breathing two-seat aerobatic airplane powered by a Russian 400-horsepower Vedeneyev M14P radial engine.

QUICKSILVER MX-2

Manufacturer
Eipper Formance/
Eipper Aircraft/
Quicksilver (USA)

Year introduced
1977

Number built 14,000+

Wingspan 28 feet (8.5 m)

Length 18 feet, 1 inch (5.5 m)

Height 8 feet, 10 inches (2.5 m)

Useful load (includes fuel) 275 pounds (124.75 kg)

Maximum takeoff weight 525 pounds (238.25 kg)

Top speed 54 miles per hour (87 km/h)

Engine Rotax 447 with 40 horsepower

Number of seats two

Range as far as your neighbor's pasture on a summer evening

Facts of note
Ultralights grew from the foot-launched hang-gliding movement. It was reasoned that adding a small engine and propeller could sustain gliding flight. Later, designers added seats and wheels.

It was the ultralight community that first introduced a ballistic full-aircraft parachute. In the event of a structural failure, the pilot could fire off a rocket that would propel a parachute canopy outward and gently lower pilot and aircraft to earth. The idea has evolved to include light passenger aircraft such as the Cirrus line of four-seat single pistons—even the developmental Cirrus jet is said to include provisions for a full-aircraft parachute system.

ROBINSON R22

Manufacturer
Robinson Helicopters
(USA)

Year introduced
1979

Number built
4,500+

Rotor diameter 25 feet, 2 inches (7.5 m)

Length 28 feet, 8 inches (8.5 m)

Height 8 feet, 11 inches (2.5 m)

Useful load (includes fuel) 574 pounds (260.25 kg)

Maximum takeoff weight 1,370 pounds (621.5 kg)

Top speed 117 miles per hour (188.25 km/h)

Engine Lycoming O-320 with 124 horsepower

Number of seats two

Range 240 miles (386.25 km)

Facts of note
The unique control system in the R22 consists of a single T-bar emerging from between the seats, which is accessible to either the left- or right-side occupant. Besides simplifying the control hardware, the arrangement makes entering and exiting the cabin easier.

In 1999, work began on modifying a Robinson R22 for use as a military drone. Boeing Phantom Works' Maverick and Renegade are equipped with electro-optical and infrared camera systems.

SOPWITH CAMEL

Manufacturer
Sopwith Aviation Co.
(England)

Year introduced
1917

Number built 5,490

Wingspan 28 feet
(8.5 m)

Length 18 feet, 9 inches (5.5 m)

Height 8 feet, 6 inches (2.5 m)

Useful load (includes fuel) 535 pounds (242.75 kg)

Maximum takeoff weight 1,455 pounds (660 kg)

Top speed 115 miles per hour (185 km/h)

Armament two Vickers .303-caliber machine guns

Engine various rotary engines, including the Gnome and the Clerget with 100–130 horsepower

Number of seats one

Range 300 miles (482.75 km)

Facts of note
Seven original Sopwith Camels survive, including the one flown by Flight Sub Lieutenant Stuart Culley when he shot down Zeppelin LZ100. That Camel was built by manufacturer William & Beardmore and is now on display at the Imperial War Museum in London.

One of the most famous Sopwith Camels isn't an airplane at all, but a doghouse. Charles Schulz's *Peanuts* character Snoopy fancies himself a World War I ace, and as his alter ego, curses the Red Baron every time his Camel returns from combat filled with holes.

SPACE SHUTTLE

Manufacturer
Rockwell
International (USA)

Year introduced
1982

Number built five

Wingspan 78 feet (23.75 m)

Length 122 feet, 2 inches (37.25 m)

Height 56 feet, 6 inches (17 m)

Payload (to orbit) 30,000 pounds (13.5 mt)

Top speed 17,320 miles per hour (27,873.75 km/h)

Engine solid boosters and LOX/hydrogen engines with total thrust of 7.5 million pounds (340,194 mt)

Crew seven

Facts of note
Since the Space Shuttle glided to a landing without power, there was no such thing as a balked landing.

Astronauts trained to land the Space Shuttle in a modified Gulfstream business jet.

SPAD S.XIII

Manufacturer
SPAD (France)

Year introduced
1917

Number built
8,472

Wingspan 27 feet, 1 inch (8.25 m)

Length 20 feet, 6 inches (6 m)

Height 8 feet, 7 inches (2.5 m)

Useful load (includes fuel) 618 pounds (280.25 kg)

Maximum takeoff weight 1,863 pounds (845 kg)

Top speed 135 miles per hour (217.25 kg)

Armament two Vickers .303-caliber machine guns

Engine Hispano Suiza liquid cooled V-8 with up to 220 horsepower

Number of seats one

Range 276 miles (444.25 km)

Facts of note
SPAD S.XIIIs were flown by French aces and national heroes Georges Guynemer and Rene Fonck. Americans who flew the SPAD included top-scoring former race-car driver Eddie Rickenbacker and Frank Luke, known as

the Arizona Balloon Buster because of his propensity for destroying German observation balloons.

Ray Brooks of Framingham, Massachusetts, a 1917 graduate of MIT, flew a SPAD S.XIII against the Germans in World War I, scoring six victories and making him an ace. At the end of the war, he was asked to select an example of the SPAD to return to the United States for display. He chose his own aircraft, Smith IV, and it now hangs in the Smithsonian Institution Air & Space Museum in Washington, D.C.

SPIRIT OF ST. LOUIS

Manufacturer
Ryan Aircraft (USA)

Year introduced
1927

Number built one

Wingspan 46 feet (14 m)

Length 27 feet, 7 inches (8.25 m)

Height 9 feet, 10 inches (2.75 m)

Useful load (including fuel) 2,985 pounds (1.25 mt)

Maximum takeoff weight 5,135 pounds (2.25 mt)

Top speed 133 miles per hour (214 km/h)

Engine Wright J5C "Whirlwind" radial with 223 horsepower

Number of seats one

Range 4,100 miles (6,598.25 km)

Facts of note
When the *Spirit of St. Louis* landed at Paris Le Bourget airfield, the crowd rushed out onto the runway to envelop Lindbergh, and much of the fuselage fabric covering was torn away for souvenirs (along with Lindbergh's original flight log). After moving it to a hangar, the French stripped the *Spirit* down and completely recovered her with new fabric as Lindbergh slept. One has to wonder what became of those purloined strips of fabric—to say nothing of the priceless, hand-written flight log.

In the months following the New York–Paris flight, Lindbergh took the *Spirit of St. Louis* on a promotional tour around the United States. Its last flight was April 28, 1928 (less than a year after the Atlantic flight), from St. Louis to Washington, D.C., where the airplane was retired and remains on display at the Smithsonian Institution National Air & Space Museum. Including more than twenty-four hours of test-flying and the thirty-three-hour flight to Paris, the *Spirit* logged a total of 489 hours—and all but one was flown by Lindbergh. His old barnstorming pal Bud Gurney was allowed to fly one short hop and is the only other pilot in history to have flown the iconic plane.

SUKHOI SU-27

Manufacturer
Sukhoi (Russia)

Year introduced
1984

Number built 680

Wingspan 48 feet, 3 inches (14.75 m)

Length 72 feet (22 m)

Height 19 feet, 6 inches (5.75 m)

Useful load (includes fuel and armaments) 15,550 pounds (7 mt)

Maximum takeoff weight 51,650 pounds (23.5 mt)

Top speed Mach 2.3 (1,750¾ miles per hour [2,817.5 km/h])

Armament one 30-mm cannon; up to 17,600 pounds (8 mt) of external ordnance on ten pylons; various complements of short- to medium-range air-to-air missiles

Engines two Saturn/Lyulka AL-31 turbofans with 16,910-pound (7.75-mt) thrust each, or 27,560-pound (12.5-mt) thrust with afterburner

Number of seats one to two

Range 2,070 miles (3,331.25 km), depending on armament payload

Facts of note
A two-seat Su-30MKI demonstrator (the export version of the Su-27 series) crashed at Paris Le Bourget Airport while practicing for the 1999 Paris Air Show. Both the pilot and rear-seat crewman ejected and were uninjured.

The original specification that led to the Su-27 series was split into two tracks in order to develop a less complex, less expensive model. The result was the MiG-29, a smaller and shorter-range fighter.

SUPERMARINE SPITFIRE

Manufacturer
Supermarine (UK)

Year introduced
1938

Number built
20,000+ (all variants)

Wingspan 36 feet, 10 inches (11 m)

Length 29 feet, 11 inches (8.75 m)

Height 11 feet, 5 inches (3.25 m)

Useful load (includes fuel) 1,532 pounds (695 kg)

Maximum takeoff weight 6,622 pounds (3 mt)

Top speed 378 miles per hour (608.25 km/h)

Armament four .303-caliber machine guns

Engine Rolls-Royce Merlin V-12 45 with 1,470 horsepower

Number of seats one

Range 1,140 miles (1,834.75 km) with 470-mile (756.5-km) combat radius

Facts of note
Test pilot Joseph "Mutt" Summers flew the first flight in the Spitfire prototype, K5054. When he landed after the eight-minute flight, he shouted, "Don't touch a thing!," which has been misinterpreted to mean that the airplane flew perfectly. What he really meant was that he wanted all the adjustments and settings recorded for his baseline evaluation, and he didn't want anything changed before he had established where everything stood.

RAF Group Captain Harry Broadhurst established himself during the Battle of Britain, and when Supermarine developed the Spitfire Mk IX, he convinced them to let him take one of the test aircraft up for a hop. What he didn't tell them was he was taking it across the Channel to fly over German-held territory. Broadhurst was unfamiliar with the Mk IX's two-stage supercharger, and when the second stage kicked in at altitude over France, there was a loud banging sound, which was perfectly normal, but unexpected. He dodged violently, thinking he was under attack. In telling the story after the war, he said, "I thought some brute of a Hun had started offloading ammunition at me."

TBM 850

Manufacturer
Daher Socata (France)

Year introduced
1990

Number built 600+
(all variants: 850 still in production)

Wingspan 41 feet, 7 inches (12.5 kg)

Length 34 feet, 11 inches (10.25 m)

Height 14 feet, 3 inches (4.25 m)

Useful load (includes fuel) 2,695 pounds (1.25 mt)

Maximum takeoff weight 7,394 pounds (3.25 mt)

Top speed 368 miles per hour (592.25 km/h)

Engine Pratt & Whitney Canada PT6A-66C with 850-shaft horsepower

Number of passenger seats four to six

Range 1,784 miles (2,871 km)

Facts of note
What's in a name? In the case of the TBM series, TB stands for Tarbes, the French city that was home base for Socata, and M is for Mooney. The TBM 850's competition is stiff. It includes the Swiss Pilatus PC-12 and the American Piper Meridian.

TBM operators include the French Army and Air Force. Equipped with a large cargo door, the airplane also makes an effective package delivery platform.

VAN'S RV3

Manufacturer
Vans Aircraft (USA)

Year introduced
1974

Number built
275+

Wingspan 19 feet, 11 inches (5.75 m)

Length 19 feet (5.75 m)

Height 5 feet (1.5 m)

Useful load (includes fuel) 350 pounds (158.75 kg)

Maximum takeoff weight 1,100 pounds (499 kg)

Top speed 207 miles per hour (333 km/h)

Engine usually Lycoming, 100–160 horsepower

Number of seats one

Range 595 miles (957.5 km)

Facts of note
In 2012, a group of Van's Aircraft enthusiasts completed restoring a RV-1 and flew it on a tour around the country, ending up in Oshkosh, Wisconsin, where the airplane is on proud display at the Experimental Aircraft Association Museum.

RV-series creator VanGrunsven's designs are often inspired by requests from potential customers, or RV builders who want something different. The RV-4 was a tandem, two-seat version of the RV-3; RV-6 was his first side-by-side design; the RV-8 has a larger cockpit (for larger pilots) and a sliding bubble canopy; and the RV-10 was his first four-seater.

VOUGHT F4U CORSAIR

Manufacturer
Vought (USA)

Year introduced
late 1942

Number built
12,571 (all variants)

Wingspan 41 feet (12.5 m)

Length 31 feet, 8 inches (9.5 m)

Height 14 feet, 9 inches (4.25 m)

Useful load (includes fuel) 5,465 pounds (2.5 mt)

Maximum takeoff weight 14,670 pounds (6.75 mt)

Top speed 443 miles per hour (713 km/h)

Armament six .50-caliber machine guns, hard points for bombs and rockets

Engine Pratt & Whitney R2800 with 2,325 horsepower

Number of seats one

Range 897 miles (1,443.5 km) without drop tanks

Facts of note
During World War II, Charles Lindbergh visited Corsair combat squadrons in the Pacific as a factory

representative for Vought Aircraft. Though in his forties at the time, he flew with fighter pilots half his age, showing them the leaning techniques he used on his New York–Paris flight in 1927. Many a Corsair pilot had Lindbergh's technique to thank for getting them home after a long mission by stretching fuel consumption.

The Corsair's most distinguishing characteristic is its inverted gull bent-wing design. While part of the purpose was to shorten the landing-gear legs for punishing carrier operations, there was an aerodynamic benefit to the design, as well. The least aerodynamically disruptive way to join wing and fuselage is exactly 90 degrees—so with a round fuselage, the best design is either a mid-wing or the inverted gull wing, as found on the Corsair.

VOYAGER

Manufacturer
Voyager Aircraft/
Rutan Aircraft
Factory (USA)

Year introduced
1986

Number built one

Wingspan 110 feet, 8 inches (33.5 m)

Length 29 feet, 2 inches (8.75 m)

Height 10 feet, 2 inches (3 m)

Fuel capacity Approximately 1,168½ gallons (4,423.25 L) in seventeen separate tanks

Empty weight 2,250 pounds (1 mt)

Maximum takeoff weight 9,694½ pounds (4.5 mt)

Cruise speed 122 miles per hour (196.25 kmh)

Engines Continental O-240 (front); liquid-cooled Continental IOL-200 (rear)

Number of seats two

Range 24,986 miles (40,211 km)

Facts of note
The Voyager touched down to wild fanfare, with more than 55,000 spectators. It is now on view at the National Air & Space Museum in Washington, D.C.

Pilots Dick Rutan and Jeana Yeager were the first to use Bose active noise-canceling headsets, developed by Dr. Ahmed Bose specifically for the flight.

WRIGHT FLYER

Manufacturer
Wright Brothers
(USA)

Year introduced
1903

Number built one

Wingspan 40 feet,
4 inches (12.25 m)

Length 21 feet,
1 inch (6.5 m)

Height 9 feet (2.75 m)

Useful load (includes fuel) 140 pound (63.5 kg)

Maximum takeoff weight 745 pounds (338 kg)

Top speed 30 miles per hour (48.25 km/h)

Engine four-cylinder, liquid cooled with 12 horsepower; designed by Charles Taylor

Number of seats one

Range 852 feet (259.75 m) flown during its last of four flights on Dec. 17, 1903

Facts of note
To launch later versions of their aircraft, the Wrights used a catapult. This can be seen in films of their later flights. But the first four flights of the *Flyer* were made from a standing start.

The Wrights were meticulous in filing for patents on their flying machine, especially when it came to their method of wing-warping for roll control. This led to protracted court battles with Glenn Curtiss, who claimed the small extra surfaces at the trailing edges of his planes' wings—ailerons—were a new invention, and thus not subject to the restrictions of the Wright patent.

YAKOVLEV YAK-9

Manufacturer
Yakovlev (Soviet Union)

Year introduced
1942

Number built
16,769

Wingspan
31 feet, 11 inches (9.5 m)

Length 28 feet (8.5 m)

Height 9 feet, 10 inches (2.75 m)

Useful load (includes fuel) 1,688 pounds (765.75 kg)

Maximum takeoff weight 6,858 pounds (3 mt)

Top speed 367 miles per hour (590.5 km/h)

Armament two 12.7-mm machine guns; one 20-mm cannon

Engine Klimov M-105 V-12 with 1,180 horsepower

Number of seats one

Range 845 miles (1,360 km)

Facts of note
Besides Russia, nine different countries operated Yak-9s, including France. The Normandy-Niemen of l'Armée de l'Air squadron used them.

Reproduction Yak-9s are currently being built using American Allison V-12 engines in place of the original Russian Klimov powerplants.

weldon**owen**

President, CEO Terry Newell
VP, Sales Amy Kaneko
VP, Publisher Roger Shaw
Creative Director Kelly Booth
Senior Editor Lucie Parker
Project Editor Emelie Griffin
Project Art Director Iain Morris
Designers Meghan Hildebrand, Suzi Hutsell
Image Coordinator Conor Buckley
Production Director Chris Hemesath
Production Manager Michelle Duggan

© 2013 Weldon Owen International
1150 Brickyard Cove Road
Richmond, CA 94801
www.weldonowen.com

Library of Congress Control Number: 2013948552

ISBN 13: 978-1-61628-606-4

12 11 10 9 8
2020 2021 2022 2023 2024

Printed in China.

Publisher Acknowledgments
Flight: 100 Greatest Aircraft would not be possible without
the immense talent, extraordinary expertise, and considerable
good spirits of our author, Mark Phelps, and our cohorts at
Flying magazine: Robert Goyer, Bethany Whitfield, Stephen
Pope, and Pia Bergqvist.

Additional gratitude is owed Jacqueline Aaron, Ian Cannon,
Scott Erwert, Bridget Fitzgerald, Laura Harger, Rachel Lopez
Metzger, and Marisa Solís.

AUTHOR ACKNOWLEDGMENTS

First, let me thank my friend and *Flying* Editor-in-Chief Robert
Goyer for his confidence in giving me the opportunity to take on
this daunting project. I also have to thank former *Flying* publisher
Dick Koenig for being one of my strongest advocates over many
years. And there is no way to repay *Flying* Managing Editor
Bethany Whitfield for her long hours' making sure this book came
out as well as it did. Naturally, the team at Weldon Owen deserves
praise, especially Roger Shaw and Lucie Parker. I'd also like to
go way back in time and thank Richard L. Collins for getting me
started in this crazy business when he hired me to come work at
Flying so many years ago. For inspiration, I have to commend all
the other writers, pilots, aircraft designers, and other visionaries
throughout history who have brought aviation to where it is today,
and who continue looking skyward to the future.

Finally, I cannot thank my wife, Leslie, and sons Marcus and Elijah
enough for their love and affection—and for tiptoeing past the door
to my office as I worked those late-night shifts on this book.

PHOTO CREDITS

Airbus: 18 **Alamy:** 70-71, 94-95, 102-103, 111, 115, 130-131, 136-137, 209 **Joerg Amann:** 155 **EAA Archives/The Spirit of Aviation:** 7 (right), 26-27, 88, 97, 114, 138, 160, 181, 198-199, 216, 235 **Ian Beatty:** 161, 223 **Jay Beckman:** 24-25, 76-77, 120-121, 125, 132-133, 170, 186-187, 202-203 **Boeing:** 41-42, 175 **Paul Bowen:** 156 **Cessna Aircraft Company:** 34, 90, 119, 144, 220 **Gavin Conroy:** 48-49, 108 **Corbis:** 101, 225 **Dassault Falcon:** 80-81 **Karl Drage:** 109, 217 **Embraer:** 196-197 *Flying* magazine: 78-79, 226 **Robert Goyer:** 46-47, 52-53, 73, 144, 145, 154, 168-169, 220, 232 **Gulfstream Aerospace Corporation:** 96

Jim Koepnick: 20, 231 **James Lawrence:** 208, 215 **Phil Makanna:** 56-57, 75, 106, 173 **NASA:** 134 (Armstrong), 152, 233 **Derek Pedley:** 59 **Piaggio Aero Industries:** 140-141 **Pilatus Aircraft:** 188-189 **Jim Raeder:** 166, 180 **Rod Reilly:** 16-17, 21-23, 67-69, 91, 124, 177 **Rhinebeck Aerodrome/ Gilles Auliard:** 128 **Brian Silcox:** 35, 38-39, 104-105, 126, 142-143, 172, 206 **The Gordon S. Williams Collection/The Museum of Flight:** 178-179 **The Peter M. Bowers Collection/The Museum of Flight:** 2-3, 28-29, 100, 139 **The Lear Collection/The Museum of Flight:** 62-62 **The Museum of Flight Collection:** 74, 86-87, 112-113, 167,

190-191, 229 **Shutterstock Images:** 1, 4-6, 7 (left), 8, 12-13, 19, 30-31, 36-37, 42-45, 48-51, 54-55, 58, 60, 66, 82, 85, 89, 92-93, 98-99, 107, 110, 116, 118, 129, 148-151, 153, 157, 164-165, 174, 176, 182, 184-185, 200-201, 204-205, 207, 212-213, 219, 240, cover, endpapers **Scott Slocum:** 72, 83, 127, 146-147, 171, 219, 239 **U.S. Air Force:** 61, 117, 133 (Lindborgh, Doolittle, Davis, Yeager), 158-159, 192-193 **U.S. Department of Defense:** 84, 183 **U.S. Library of Congress:** 15-16 **Wiki user Richard Author Norton:** 133 (Rodgers) **Wiki user Viniciusmc:** 133 (Bader) **Wiki**

user BetacommandBot: 134 (Earhart) **Wiki user Clindberg:** 134 (Sullenberger) **Wiki user FA2010:** 194 (Montgolfier) **Wiki user Howcheng:** 194 (Lilienthal) **Wiki user OldakQuill:** 194 (da Vinci) **Wiki user Huntster:** 195 (Virgin) **Wiki user Magnus Manske:** 195 (Wingsuit) **Wiki user Pazmany:** 195 (Piper) **Wiki user Russavia:** 195 (de Havilland)

ILLUSTRATIONS

Conor Buckley: 9-10, 32-33, 64-65, 162-163, 194-195 **Hayden Foell:** 214-23